PREACH FOR A YEAR #3

Books by Roger Campbell

Preach for a Year #1
Preach for a Year #2
Preach for a Year #3
Preach for a Year #4
Preach for a Year #5
Preach for a Year #6
Staying Positive in a Negative World
You Can Win! No Losers in God's Family
Weight: A Better Way to Lose

PREACH
FOR A
YEAR #3

104 Sermon Outlines
Two complete outlines for every Sunday of the year

Roger Campbell

krēgel
PUBLICATIONS

Grand Rapids, MI 49501

Preach for a Year #3 by Roger F. Campbell

Copyright © 1995 by Kregel Publications, a division of Kregel, Inc., P.O. Box 2607, Grand Rapids, MI 49501. Kregel Publications provides trusted, biblical publications for Christian growth and service. Your comments and suggestions are valued.

Library of Congress Cataloging-in-Publication Data
Campbell, Roger F., 1930–
Preach for a year #3 / by Roger F. Campbell.
     p. cm.
   1. Sermons—Outlines, syllabi, etc. I. Title.
BV4223.C33 1995
251'.02—dc20
87-29400

ISBN 0-8254-2321-x

5 6 7 8 9 / 07 06 05 04 03

Printed in the United States of America

To my wife, Pauline, who has heard my sermons for more than four decades and who has prayed for me in the development and delivery of all of them.

CONTENTS

INTRODUCTION

I am deeply grateful for the opportunity of sharing this third book of sermon outlines with you. These are not just outlines prepared to publish; they have each been a special part of my pastoral life. They are road tested, and just placing them in this book brings back memories of pleasant prayer and study when they were originally prepared and of people who were affected by them.

A preacher is not so much a builder of sermons as he is a builder of people; to build people into what God wants them to be, he must love them. It is not enough to love to preach; we must love those to whom we preach.

Without love, preaching is just noise (1 Cor. 13:1).

A young minister told me he was discouraged and didn't think his preaching was getting through.

"Do you love the people?" I asked.

"I think so," he replied.

"Try looking at all of the people before you and asking God to enable you to love each one of them," I advised.

I was simply sharing what I have done repeatedly, knowing that all of my preparation and preaching would be ineffective without love.

The love of God is the heart of our message and the central theme of these sermon outlines. If at the end of the year you and your congregation love the Lord, each other, and lost people more than at the beginning, my prayers for this book will have been answered.

"Beloved, if God so loved us, we ought also to love one another" (1 John 4:11).

ROGER CAMPBELL

A Year to Build

                       Acts 4:19–23

I. Introduction
  A. *An Exciting Time to Be a Part of This Church!*
   1. A church where people love one another
   2. A church that has known past blessings
   3. A church in an area where many need Christ
  B. *Time to Look Ahead with Confidence*
   1. A time to expect the best
   2. A time to build for the future
  C. *How Shall We Build?*

II. Body
  A. *Let Us Build through Evangelism (vv. 19–21)*
   1. Paul stoned and believed dead
    a. The disciples gather around his body
    b. He rises and surprises them
    c. Let the world know we are alive
   2. Paul heads for Derbe to reach souls
    a. This was the purpose of his life (1 Cor. 9:16)
    b. This was what made him a missionary
    c. This was why he founded so many churches
   3. Evangelism is vital to our existence as a church
    a. Let us bring in people to hear the Gospel
    b. Let us be living messengers of the Gospel
    c. Let us always preach the Gospel (Mark 16:15)
  B. *Let Us Build through Exhortation (vv. 21–22)*
   1. To exhort is to encourage
   2. Paul taught those who received the Gospel
   3. He encouraged all believers to greater faith
    a. Let's encourage those who are discouraged
    b. Let's encourage those who feel like giving up
    c. Let's encourage our own families
    d. Let's encourage those in leadership
    e. Let's encourage all in the family of faith
   4. Be encouraged and be an encourager
  C. *Let Us Build through Edification (v. 23)*
   1. To edify is to build up
   2. Some specialize in tearing down

a. Refuse to be part of their wrecking crew
b. Be a builder, not a destroyer
3. Paul building up believers
   a. Organizing the churches
   b. Giving responsibilities to leaders
   c. Praying with and for those he won to Christ

III. Conclusion
A. *A Great Year to Build!*
B. *Here Are the Materials Needed: Evangelism, Exhortation, Edification*
C. *Let Us Rise Up and Build*

Follow Me

Matthew 4:18–22

I. Introduction
   A. *Thirty Years Condensed to Four Chapters*
      1. The birth in Bethlehem; the flight into Egypt
      2. The return to Nazareth; the silent years
      3. John the Baptist; the baptism; the Temptation
   B. *A New Beginning: The Earthly Ministry of Jesus*
      1. Choosing the first disciples
      2. "Follow me" (v. 19)
      3. Peter's lessons from this recurring call

II. Body
   A. *The "Follow Me" of Faith (v. 19)*
      1. Peter and Andrew busy at their daily work
         a. Making a living; providing for their families
         b. May have been struggling with problems
      2. Jesus comes where they are working
         a. He meets us where we are
         b. He meets us in our times of need
      3. Their hearts had been prepared for His call
         a. Have you heard the "Follow Me" of faith?
         b. Have you responded to His call (Rom. 5:1; Eph. 2:8–9)?
      4. The Christian life begins and continues in faith
         a. "The just shall live by faith" (Rom. 1:17)
         b. Faith overcomes the world (1 John 5:4)
         c. As faith increases, fear decreases
   B. *The "Follow Me" of Fishing for Men (v. 19)*
      1. The neglected call: Personal Evangelism
      2. The results of neglect
         a. Few churches filled
         b. Many joyless believers
      3. The cure for neglect
         a. Joy in sowing and reaping (Ps. 126:5–6)
         b. Converts bring joy (1 Thess. 2:19–20)
      4. We must get past programs to people
   C. *The "Follow Me" of Full Surrender (Matt. 16:24)*
      1. Peter rebels at the news of the cross (v. 21)

    2. The Lord's call to self-denial
    3. How this call affects us today
       a. Self-denial still in Christ's call
       b. Full surrender brings complete victory

  D. *The "Follow Me" of Focusing on Jesus (John 21:22)*
    1. Peter learns what he will do for Christ (vv. 15–19)
    2. He wonders what John will do (v. 21)
    3. Our Lord's answer to Peter
       a. What is that to thee?
       b. Follow thou me

III. Conclusion
  A. *What Is Your Response to the Lord's Call?*
  B. *Will You Decide to Follow Jesus All the Way?*
  C. *What a Great Way to Begin the New Year!*

The Great Commission

Series on Missions *Matthew 28:16–20*

I. **Introduction**
   A. *An Appointment with Jesus (v. 16)*
      1. The disciples had an appointment with Jesus
      2. We all have an appointment with Jesus (Rom. 14:12)
   B. *The Purpose of the Appointment: The Great Commission*
      1. It has sent missionaries around the world
      2. How will we respond to it today?

II. **Body**
   A. *The Great Commission Reveals a Savior with All Power: "All power is given unto me in heaven and in earth" (v. 18)*
      1. The Gospel has both earthly and heavenly dimensions
         a. We share the good news with earthly people
            (1) Facing earthly problems
            (2) Having earthly sicknesses and sorrows
         b. We say there are heavenly consequences
            (1) Sins can be forgiven
            (2) When you die you can go to heaven
      2. The Savior with power to save (Rom. 1:16)
   B. *The Great Commission Reveals a Savior for All People: "Go ye therefore, and teach all nations" (v. 19)*
      1. What an immense task!
         a. A few disciples with a world to reach
         b. They had none of our means of communication
         c. They were faithful and spread the good news everywhere
      2. Salvation for all people
         a. No people too sinful to be saved
         b. No people too backward to be saved
         c. All people need to be saved (Rom. 3:23; 6:23)
      3. Baptism for all who come to faith in Christ
         a. Those converted on Pentecost were baptized (Acts 2:41)

17

  b. The influential Ethiopian was baptized
   (Acts 8:36–38)
  c. Educated and Religious Paul was Baptized
   (Acts 9:18)
  d. Moral and merciful Cornelius was baptized
   (Acts 10:48)
 4. Bible teaching for all people
  a. "Teaching them to observe all things"
  b. Bible teaching is vital for Christian growth
C. *The Great Commission Reveals a Savior for All Time:*
 "Lo, I am with you alway" (v. 20)
 1. Jesus is sufficient for all problems in all ages
  a. The persecutions facing the disciples
  b. Jesus would be with them through them all
 2. A message that is always timely ("Unto the end of
  the world")

III. Conclusion
 A. *Are You Willing to Take This Good News to Others?*
 B. *The Mission Field Begins at Our Door*

What's Being a Missionary All About?

Series on Missions   *Mark 16:15*

I. **Introduction**
   A. *Missionary Work and Local Churches*
      1. Most churches have some interest in missions
      2. Some take great pride in their missionary programs
         a. Missionary conferences, budgets, maps, etc.
         b. Prayer for missions, giving to missions, going on missionary trips to learn and participate
   B. *But What Is a Missionary?*
      1. Missionaries are not a special class of Christians
      2. Missionaries are believers who take the Gospel to others
      3. We are all to be missionaries

II. **Body**
   A. *Missionary Work Is about Going into All the World*
      1. The last words of Jesus to His disciples were about going
         a. "Go and teach all nations" (Matt. 28:18–20)
         b. "Go ye into all the world" (Mark 16:15)
         c. "Ye shall be witnesses unto me" (Acts 1:8)
      2. Why then do so few go?
         a. Easier to serve on a board or teach than to go
         b. Easier to give money than to go
         c. Easier to preach than to go
      3. But Jesus said we are to go into all the world
      4. The world is our mission field (Matt. 13:38)
      5. The world includes every contact of every day
   B. *Missionary Work Is about Preaching the Gospel*
      1. Missionary work is sharing the Gospel (1 Cor. 15:3–4)
         a. That Christ died for our sins according to the Scriptures
         b. That He was buried and rose again
      2. Missionary work then is about God's love
         a. Forgiveness of sins because God loves us (Col. 1:14)

      b. Eternal life because God loves us (John 3:16;
        5:24)

      c. Changed lives because God loves us
        (2 Cor. 5:17)

  C. *Missionary Work Is about Reaching All People*

    1. No racial prejudice in missions
      (John 4:7; Acts 8:27)

    2. No social discrimination in missions
      (Luke 7:36–50)

    3. No age discrimination in missions
      (Matt. 19:13–15)

    4. All people are lost and need salvation
      (Rom. 3:10–23)

    5. Christ died for all (Isa. 53:6)

III. Conclusion

  A. *What Are You Going to Do to Fulfill Your Mission?*

  B. *To Whom Will You Go with the Gospel Today?*

Love Missions

1 Corinthians 13:1–3

I. Introduction

 A. Missionary Work Should Have a Vital Role in Every Church
  1. We must pray earnestly for missions
  2. We must pay the way for those called to missions
  3. We must send people from our churches to serve in missions

 B. Missionary Work Is a Work of Love
  1. Missionaries carry a message of love
  2. The Gospel is God's great love story
  3. The Bible is God's love letter to us all

II. Body

 A. To Love Missions Is to Love People (v. 1)
  1. The danger of becoming mechanical about missions
  2. We may focus only on outward things
   a. Missionary things: maps, conferences, curios
   b. Information about missions: customs, problems, etc.
  3. Missionary work without loving people is worthless
   a. Missionary strategy without love
   b. Missionary journeys without love
  4. Missionaries, at home or abroad, must love people
   a. Without love all missionary effort is fruitless
   b. Without love all missionary teaching is just noise

 B. To Love Missions Is to Love Souls
  1. Some love people but care only for outward needs
   a. Food, housing, clothing, education
   b. Meeting physical needs is important but not everything
   c. People can be well cared for and go to hell
  2. Jesus stressed the importance of the soul (Mark 8:36)

    3. Missions should major on reaching people for Christ

    4. Who cares if a sinner goes to hell?

      a. The Father cares and sent His Son

      b. The Son cares and came to die for sinners

      c. The Holy Spirit cares and calls sinners to repentance

      d. What about you and me?

  C. *To Love Missions Is to Love Jesus*

    1. "If you love me keep my commandments" (John 14:15)

    2. The great commission (Matt. 28:18–20)

    3. Our Lord calls us witnesses (Acts 1:8)

    4. Do you love Jesus enough to tell others of His love?

III. Conclusion

  A. *What Part Does Love Play in Your Missionary Vision?*

    1. Do you love people?

    2. Do you love souls?

    3. Do you love Jesus?

  B. *How Will You Demonstrate Your Love in Missionary Service?*

A Mighty Missionary Church

Series on Missions   *Acts 11:19–30; 13:1–5*

I. **Introduction**
   A. *The Dynamic Church at Antioch*
      1. The second capital of Christianity
      2. The greatest missionary church in the New Testament
   B. *How Should We Regard the Church at Antioch?*
      1. Ought to study its success in missions
      2. Ought to implement its practices

II. **Body**
   A. *It Was a Spiritual Church (11:19–30)*
      1. How the church at Antioch was born (v. 19)
         a. Believers scattered because of persecution
         b. Stephen's martyrdom fresh on their minds
         c. Evangelism alive in Antioch (v. 21)
      2. Spiritual in its reputation
         a. The good news reached Jerusalem (v. 22)
         b. Barnabas arrives to teach the new converts (v. 22)
         c. Barnabas sees that God is at work (v. 23)
      3. Spiritual in its teaching
         a. The leadership was led of the Spirit (v. 24)
         b. Paul comes to join the teaching staff (v. 25–26)
      4. Spiritual in the lives of the people
         a. Church gatherings packed with eager learners (v. 26)
         b. The world called them *"Christians"* (v. 26)
   B. *It Was a Serving Church (13:1–2)*
      1. A church with gifted teachers
      2. The leaders ministered to the Lord (v. 2)
         a. Teaching the Word
         b. Developing new converts
         c. Fasting and praying
      3. Their hearts were open to the leading of the Lord

        a. "Separate me Barnabas and Saul"
        b. God called some of their number to serve
  C. *It Was a Sending Church (vv. 2–5)*
    1. The great sending service
        a. They obeyed God's choice for Barnabas and Saul
        b. They fasted and prayed for them
        c. They laid their hands upon them
        d. They sent them away
    2. Sometimes difficult for churches to send
        a. We are better at gathering than sending
        b. We want to keep gifted people with us
        c. Sending is an act of faith and brings blessings

III. Conclusion
  A. *Each Church Should Be Developing Missionaries*
  B. *Each Church Should Be Sending Choice Servants as Missionaries*
  C. *Are We Willing to Become a Missionary Church?*

The Day of Good Tidings

Series on Missions   *2 Kings 7:1–11*

I. Introduction
   A. *The Siege of Samaria*
      1. Since the fall of man there have been wars
      2. Ben-Hadad, the king of Syria, sets seige to Samaria
      3. The terrible conditions inside the city
   B. *Elisha's Surprising Prophecy (v. 1)*
   C. *Missionary Lessons from Four Lepers*
      1. Outcasts from the city and society
      2. Had lived on the handouts of those passing by
      3. Their responses to the crisis are lessons for us all

II. Body
   A. *A Question of Survival: "Why sit we here until we die?" (v. 3)*
      1. They needed to do nothing else to die but wait
         a. So it is with every sinner (John 3:18, 36)
         b. Does not need to commit one more sin to go to hell
         c. Indecision is a state of death
      2. Apart from God's intervention, death awaited
         a. Death if they moved or death if they stayed
         b. Lost people face death if they stay in unbelief
      3. One leper wisely analyzed the situation
         a. Why should we sit here and die?
         b. God's cry to sinners: "Why will you die?" (Ezek. 18:31)
   B. *A Statement of Surrender: "Let us fall into the host of the Syrians" (v. 4)*
      1. The lepers decide to take action
      2. The risk in surrender: only a different death
      3. The hope in surrender: life
      4. Surrender saved their lives
      5. You need to surrender to Christ
         a. The risk: yourself
         b. The hope: eternal life
         c. The promise: surrender will save your life

25

C. *The Call for Sharing (vv. 9–11)*
1. Surprise! the enemy had been defeated
2. Satan was defeated at the cross
   a. Jesus suffered and died outside the city
   b. The victory has already been won
3. The lepers find life
   a. Food, silver, and gold
   b. Then the awakening: "We do not well" (v. 9)
4. The lepers share the good tidings and the city is saved

III. Conclusion
A. *This Is also a Day of Good Tidings*
1. Salvation has been provided at the cross
2. Eternal life is offered to all to trust in Jesus
B. *We Do Not Well If We Hold Our Peace*

Harvest Time

Series on Missions   *John 4:34–38*

I. **Introduction**
  A. *A Chapter of Surprises*
    1. A woman surprised that Jesus spoke to her (v. 9)
    2. A woman surprised that Jesus knew all about her (v. 39)
    3. The disciples surprised that Jesus was not hungry (vv. 31–34)
    4. The city of Sychar surprised by the changed woman (vv. 40–42)
  B. *Our Lord's Surprising Message about the Harvest*
    1. It's ready to reap
    2. Reapers are needed
    3. There are rewards for reapers

II. **Body**
  A. *The Ready Harvest (v. 35)*
    1. Confusion about the time of the harvest
      a. Not four months from now
      b. Today is the day of salvation (2 Cor. 6:2)
    2. Getting motivated for the harvest
      a. Lift up your eyes; see people around you
      b. Look on the fields; see them ripe for harvest
      c. Ask the Lord to help you see the harvest through His eyes
    3. Why the harvest is ready
      a. People everywhere are troubled
      b. The world is morally adrift
      c. Religiously the world is bewildered
  B. *The Reapers Needed for the Harvest (v. 36).*
    1. The joy of working in an abundant harvest
    2. Most do not expect to harvest today
      a. Just holding on until Jesus comes
      b. Very little witnessing, soulwinning
    3. The laborers are few (Luke 10:2)
      a. We must pray for laborers
      b. We must become laborers
    4. What are you doing in God's great harvest?

27

  C. *The Rewards Promised to Reapers in the Harvest:*
   "He that reapeth receiveth wages" (vv. 36–37)
   1. There are wages now: rejoicing (v. 36)
   2. There will be wages later (Rev. 22:12)
    a. These wages surpass any now known
    b. These are wages of eternal value
    c. His "Well done!" will be our greatest reward

III. Conclusion
  A. *Who Will Now Work in the Lord's Harvest?*
  B. *Were You Once More Involved in the Harvest than*
   Today?
  C. *Get Busy in the Harvest without Delay*

Fellowship, Joy, and Forgiveness

Series on 1 John   *1 John 1:1–10*

I. Introduction
   A. A Letter to the Family of God
      1. Warm, loving and devotional
      2. Deals with sin in the lives of believers
      3. Shows the inconsistency of being loved and not loving
   B. John's Goals as He Begins His Letter
      1. Fellowship with God and His family
      2. Fullness of joy
      3. Forgiveness of sins

II. Body
   A. Fellowship with God and His Family (vv. 1–3)
      1. John and beginnings
         a. "In the beginning was the Word" (John 1:1)
         b. "That which was from the beginning" (v. 1)
      2. John was an eyewitness
         a. "We have heard"
         b. "We have seen"
         c. "We have looked upon"
         d. "Our hands have handled"
      3. This eyewitness now gives his testimony
      4. Fellowship with God and His family (v. 3)
         a. Fellowship with God is the purpose of life
         b. Fellowship with believers deepens our walk with God
         c. "So glad I'm a part of the family of God"
   B. Fullness of Joy (v. 4)
      1. The human desire for happiness
         a. Happiness depends of the happenings of life
         b. Joy is better
         c. Joy is a spring within, whatever happens
      2. Believers are to have the joy of the Lord
         a. This is God's will for us (John 15:11)
         b. Do you have the joy of the Lord?

      3. Hindrances to fullness of joy
        a. Lack of full dedication (John 15:7)
        b. Lack of fruitfulness (John 15:8)
        c. Lack of love for others (John 15:12–17)
    C. *Forgiveness of Sin (vv. 5–10)*
      1. Contrasting light and darkness (vv. 5–7)
      2. The goal is to walk in the light (v. 7)
      3. All fall short of that goal (v. 8)
      4. When we fail, forgiveness is available:
        a. "If we confess our sins" (v. 9)
        b. "He is faithful and just to forgive" (v. 9)
      5. Confession and cleansing to be our daily experience

III. Conclusion
    A. *Fellowship, Joy, and Forgiveness All Ours in Christ*
    B. *Let Us Love the One Who First Loved Us*
    C. *Let Us also Love His Family*

Our Advocate

1 John 2:1–2

I. **Introduction**
   A. *The Purpose of This Epistle Is the Abundant Life*
      1. Fellowship with God and His family
      2. Fullness of joy, flowing from assurance of salvation
      3. Forgiveness of sin in daily life
   B. *The Problem of Sin in the Lives of Believers*
      1. Sin destroys fellowship (ch. 1)
      2. Sin will make us ashamed at Christ's coming (2:28)
      3. Sin may bring physical death (5:16)
   C. *God's Provision for Daily Victory*

II. **Body**
   A. *The Aim in the Christian Life (v. 1)*
      1. "That you sin not"
      2. Awareness of sin brings us to the Savior
         a. Want to be saved? Acknowledge you are lost
         b. Want to go to heaven? Realize you are bound for hell
         c. Christ came to save sinners
      3. Upon receiving Christ by faith we are forgiven (Col. 1:14)
      4. What should then be our goal as believers?
         a. We should aim for daily victory
         b. Jesus is our example
      5. We are equipped to win
   B. *The Advocate for All Christians (v. 1)*
      1. "But if any man sin"
         a. Facing the reality of imperfection
         b. God loves us still (Rom. 8:38–39)
      2. "We have an advocate with the Father"
         a. An advocate who comes to our aid when we stumble
         b. An advocate who intercedes in heaven for us (Heb. 7:25)

31

       c. An advocate on earth and One in heaven (John 14–16)

       d. An advocate when the Enemy comes against us

  C. *The Atonement*
1. He is the propitiation for our sins
2. He has paid for our sins with His own blood
3. Christ has reconciled us to our Father (2 Cor. 5:17–20)
4. He finished His work of reconciliation on the cross
5. His work as our advocate continues

III. Conclusion
  A. *We Are to Invite Others to the Abundant Life*
  B. *The Call for Consistent Christian Living*
1. In view of His atonement
2. In view of His continuing work as our advocate

From Profession to Perfection

Series on 1 John   *1 John 2:6*

I. **Introduction**
  A. *The Christian Life Begins with New Birth*
    1. "My little children" (v. 1)
    2. We are born again through faith in Christ (John 3:1–16)
  B. *God Wants Us to Be Confident of Our Salvation*
    1. *Know* is found forty times in this epistle
    2. The joy of knowing we are the children of God
  C. *Three Words for the Family: Profession, Progression, Perfection*

II. **Body**
  A. *Profession*
    1. "He that saith he abideth in him"
    2. We downplay the importance of profession
      a. "I'd rather see a sermon than hear one any day"
      b. Quiet faith preferred by many to zealous witnessing
    3. We are to give testimony to our faith
      a. Believe and confess (Rom. 10:9)
      b. Baptism as a means of public witness
      c. Church attendance shows our priorities
    4. We are to be His witnesses (Acts 1:8)
  B. *Progression*
    1. "Ought himself also so to walk"
      a. Believers are people on the move
      b. Our walk should confirm our talk
    2. Abiding in Christ should show in our walk
    3. Parents are pleased when a child starts walking
    4. How shall we walk?
      a. Walk honestly (Rom. 13:13)
      b. Walk in the Spirit (Gal. 5:16)
      c. Walk in love (Eph. 5:2)
      d. Walk circumspectly (Eph. 5:15)
      e. Walk in faith (Col. 2:6)
      f. Walk in wisdom, redeeming the time (Col. 4:5)
    5. How are you progressing in the Christian life?

    C. *Perfection*
        1. "Even as he walked"
        2. We have a great example to follow
        3. We are not perfect, but Jesus is (1 Peter 2:21–25)
            a. Others fail, Jesus doesn't
            b. Focus on Jesus, not faults of others
        4. In looking to Jesus, we can be victorious
           (Heb. 12:2)
        5. When we meet Jesus we will be like Him
           (1 John 3:2)

III. **Conclusion**
    A. *Three Commitments to Make a Difference in Our Walk*
        1. I will not look at the faults of others
        2. I will look for evidences of Christlikeness in others
        3. I will keep looking to my perfect Savior
    B. *Let's Make These Life-Changing Commitments Today*

To Love or Not to Love? That Is the Question

Series on 1 John   *1 John 2:1–17*

I. **Introduction**
  A. *The Epistle with the Family in Mind*
    1. "My little children"
    2. "Our fellowship is with the Father and His Son Jesus Christ"
  B. *Love in Our Earthly Families*
    1. Lovers pledging their love in marriage
    2. Love continues: "Husbands love your wives" (Eph. 5:25)
  C. *John's Lessons about Love in the Family of God*

II. **Body**
  A. *John Realizing God's Love for Him (v. 5)*
    1. John and his brother James had been fishermen
      a. Worked with their father, Zebedee
      b. They loved their father, the boats, the sea
    2. Then one day John heard the call of Jesus (Mark 1:17–20)
      a. He had been mending nets
      b. Now he would become a mender of men (Luke 5:10)
    3. John learning about love
      a. Observed the compassionate Christ
      b. His great lesson of love at the cross (John 18)
      c. "The disciple whom Jesus loved" (John 21:20)
    4. God loves us all (John 3:16)
  B. *John Reasoning That He Must Love His Brother (v. 10)*
    1. The loved have an obligation to love
    2. "He that loveth his brother abideth in the light"
      a. Jesus is the light (John 8:12)
      b. Love reveals our walk with Jesus
    3. How love shows in life (1 Cor. 13:4–7)
      a. Love is patient and kind
      b. Love is not envious or proud
      c. Love is consistent, not selfish or suspicious
      d. Love is never glad when others are hurt
      e. Love is pleased when truth triumphs

       f. Love puts up with slights, insults, failures
       g. Love believes the best about others
  C. *John Refusing to Love the World (vv. 15–17)*
    1. "Love not the world" (v. 15)
      a. Does not refer to people (John 3:16)
      b. Does not refer to creation (Matt. 6:26–30)
      c. Refers to the Christ-rejecting world system—
        H. A. Ironside: "that system that man has built
        up . . . in which he is trying to make himself
        happy without God."
    2. John refuses to love "things"
    3. Lust and pride call us to love the world (v. 16)
    4. The "world" is passing away
    5. John chooses to love the One who is eternal

III. Conclusion
  A. *We Are Known by Who and What We Love*
  B. *Who and What Do You Love?*

Urgent Words to the Children

Series on 1 John   *1 John 2:28*

I. **Introduction**
   A. *John Keeps Stressing the Family Relationship*
      1. We are born into the family of God by faith
         (John 3:3–5)
      2. This is a family of love
      3. The Father's love flows through each of His
         children
   B. *John's Urgent Message to the Children*
      1. He wants them to fully enjoy the family
      2. He wants them to live like children of the Father
      3. He wants them to be a credit to their family name

II. **Body**
   A. *Abiding in Christ*
      1. "And now, little children, abide in Him"
      2. What does it mean to abide in Christ?
         a. To have fellowship with Him
         b. To experience close communion with Him
         c. To be fully surrendered to Him
         d. To live daily to please Him
      3. H. A. Ironside: "To abide in Christ is to live in
         fellowship with Him. It is one thing to be in Him
         as having life in Him, but it is another thing to
         abide in Him as enjoying communion with Him."
   B. *Abundant Living in Christ*
      1. "We may have confidence"
      2. Living confidently
         a. Having assurance of salvation
         b. Feeling comfortable with Jesus
      3. Enjoying the Father and the family
      4. Seizing each moment to rejoice in Christ and live
         for Him
      5. Jesus calls us to the abundant life (John 10:10)
      6. C. H. Spurgeon: "You shall have happier views of
         heavenly things as you climb the hill of spiritual
         experience. As you abide in Christ you shall have
         firmer confidence, richer joy, greater stability,

37

more communion with Jesus, and greater delight in the Lord your God."

C. *Avoiding Shame at Christ's Return*
1. "And not be ashamed before Him at His coming"
2. Would you have been ashamed if Jesus had returned last week?
    a. Last night?
    b. This morning?
    c. Five minutes ago?
3. What would have caused you shame?
4. Are you willing to surrender this area of life to Christ?

III. Conclusion
A. *Christ Died for Our Sins: Accept His Forgiveness*
B. *Christ Is Risen: Live in Fellowship with Him*
C. *Christ Is Coming: Live Expecting His Return*

John's Purifying Hope

1 John 3:1–3

I. **Introduction**
   A. *John's Call for Christlike Living*
      1. This call runs throughout his epistles
      2. Our text gives powerful incentives for such living
      3. These make up John's purifying hope
   B. *Why John Chose to Keep His Life Pure*

II. **Body**
   A. *He Was Amazed at the Love of God (v. 1)*
      1. "Behold what manner of love"
      2. John couldn't find words to explain God's love
         a. "God so loved the world" (John 3:16)
         b. "Behold, what manner of love (v. 1)
      3. Lessons in love for John
         a. He had been with Jesus in the upper room
         b. Jesus had washed John's feet (13:1–17)
         c. He had stood at the cross (19:25–30)
      4. John wanted to please the One who loved him
   B. *He Appreciated His Position as a Child of God (vv. 1–2)*
      1. "That we should be called the sons of God"
         a. Sinners are made into sons
         b. Another amazing thought to John
      2. A simple fisherman could be a son of God
      3. This sonship causes conflict with the world
         a. "Therefore the world knoweth us not"
         b. Christians must prepare to be misunderstood
         c. Our Lord was misunderstood and rejected (John 15:18–27)
      4. Sonship begins now!
         a. "Now are we the sons of God"
         b. Eternal life begins at the moment of new birth
   C. *He Anticipated Christ's Return When He Would Be Like Him (3:2–3)*
      1. John knew the failures of this life
         a. Like all of us, he had some regrets
         b. "If we say we have no sin, we deceive ourselves" (1:8)

2. Paul wrote of this daily struggle (Rom. 7:14–21)
3. John looked forward to a better day
   a. When the mysteries will be cleared up
   b. When we shall all be changed
      (1 Cor. 15:51–52)
   c. When we shall be like Him
   d. We shall see Him as He is
4. John wanted to be like Jesus now

III. **Conclusion**
   A. *Reviewing John's Reasons for a Pure Life*
      1. He knew God loved him
      2. He knew he was a child of God
      3. He knew at his Lord's return he would be like Him
   B. *What Moves You to Holy Living?*

Why Jesus Came

Series on 1 John   *1 John 3:5–8; 4:9*

I. **Introduction**
   A. *Questions of the Ages*
      1. Why the Incarnation?
      2. Why was Jesus born in Bethlehem's stable?
      3. Why did Jesus endure the cross?
   B. *John Gives Us the Answers*

II **Body**
   A. *He Came to Take Away Our Sins (v. 5)*
      1. "He was manifested to take away our sins"
      2. We are all sinners (Rom. 3:23)
         a. Sin brings sorrow, pain and death (Rom. 5:12)
         b. Jesus came to bring us eternal life (Rom. 6:23)
      3. Jesus loves sinners
         a. Yet He was without sin (v. 5)
         b. He is the perfect Savior
      4. Have you made Him your own?
   B. *He Came to Destroy the Works of the Devil (v. 8)*
      1. "Manifested that he might destroy the works of the devil"
      2. The work of the Devil in Eden (Gen. 3)
         a. Tempting Eve to eat the forbidden fruit (Gen. 3)
         b. Death came upon all because of sin
      3. The work of God in Eden (Gen. 3)
         a. Seeking Adam and Eve who were afraid
         b. Promising a Redeemer who would bruise the Serpent's head
      4. At the cross, the promise was fulfilled
      5. Jesus is still destroying the works of the Devil
         a. Saving those who trust in Him (John 6:37)
         b. Changing lives; making new creatures (2 Cor. 5:17)
         c. Setting those in bondage to Satan free (John 8:36)

C. *He Came to Show the Father's Love (4:9)*
   1. "Manifested the love of God toward us"
      a. God sent His Son into the world
      b. Eternal life is ours through Him
   2. God loved us first (v. 10)
      a. Loved us while were sinners (Rom. 5:8)
      b. Loved us when we rebelled against Him
   3. This love moved God to send Jesus to die for us
      a. Who can explain such love?
      b. Why would any reject such love?

III. **Conclusion**
   A. *Here Is an Invitation to Be Forgiven and Free*
   B. *Accept This Invitation of Love—and Live*

God's Great Circle of Love

1 John 4:10–11

I. **Introduction**
   A. *John the Disciple of Love*
      1. Saw himself as the recipient of Christ's love
      2. Called for believers to love one another
      3. Refused to love the world or the things in the world
   B. *John Reveals the Reach and Rationale for Love in the Christian Life*
      1. God loved us first
      2. We ought then to love one another
      3. The circle of love: from God to us to others

II. **Body**
   A. *Where Love Starts (v. 10)*
      1. Love starts with God
         a. God is love (v. 8)
         b. God loves us all (John 3:16)
      2. We have not sought God (Rom. 3:11)
         a. He has sought us
         b. God is the original seeker
         c. Finally seeking God is but responding to His love
      3. Loved from the foundation of the world
         a. Chosen in Him (Eph. 1:4)
         b. Redemption planned (1 Peter 1:18–20)
         c. The Lamb slain (Rev. 13:8)
   B. *What Love Spends (v. 10)*
      1. "The propitiation for our sins"
      2. Propitiation refers to the death of Christ on the cross
         a. Propitiation demanded full payment for our sins
         b. Jesus paid that price for us (Isa. 53:5–6)
      3. Propitiation was God settling our sin problem
      4. H. A. Ironside on propitiation: "In those hours of darkness God was dealing with His Son about that awful question, and there He bore in His inmost

43

soul the judgment that you and I would have to bear ourselves for all eternity if left without a Savior. Thus He became the propitiation."

C. *Where Love Sends (v. 11)*
  1. Receiving love brings responsibility
      a. God loves us
      b. We are therefore to love one another
  2. We are sent to all believers with love (3:14–17)
      a. This love goes beyond words
      b. We are to love in deed and truth
      c. This love produces compassion for those in need
  3. God's love also sends us to sinners with the Gospel

III. Conclusion
  A. *Have You Thanked Your Lord Today Because He Loves You?*
  B. *Have You Received Christ, the Gift of His Love?*
  C. *Are You Carrying God's Love to Others?*

The Overcoming Life

Series on 1 John   *1 John 4:4, 18; 5:4*

I. **Introduction**
   A. *No Born Losers in God's Family*
      1. Believers are equipped to win
      2. Divine resources are ours for every battle
      3. There really is victory in Jesus
   B. *Facing Three Powerful Enemies*
      1. Spiritual adversaries
      2. Recurring anxieties
      3. The world's allurements
   C. *We Can Overcome*

II. **Body**
   A. *Overcoming Our Adversaries (4:4)*
      1. Spiritual adversaries are always active (vv. 1–3)
         a. Speaking through false prophets (v. 1)
         b. The spirit of antichrist (v. 3)
      2. Our adversaries are deceptive and powerful
         a. "The wiles of the devil" (Eph. 6:11)
         b. "Principalities and powers" (Eph. 6:12)
         c. The rulers of the darkness of this world
            (Eph. 6:12)
      3. Why we can overcome these powerful adversaries
         a. The One in us is greater
         b. The Holy Spirit is the One in us
            (John 14:16–17)
         c. The believer's body is God's temple
            (1 Cor. 6:19–20)
      4. Expect to overcome
   B. *Overcoming Our Anxieties (4:18)*
      1. "There is no fear in love"
         a. Responding to God's love brings faith
         b. Faith and fear are opposites
      2. "Perfect love casteth out fear"
         a. Knowing we are loved makes us unafraid
         b. This perfect love brought Jesus to the cross
         c. Saving love is also keeping love

    3. Fear brings torment
    4. God's perfect love brings tranquility
       a. Stop being tormented by fear
       b. We overcome fear by resting in His perfect love
  C. *Overcoming the World's Allurements (5:1–4)*
    1. We are born again through faith in Christ (v. 1)
    2. New birth equips us to overcome
    3. The world holds many allurements (2:16)
       a. The lust of the flesh
       b. The lust of the eyes
       c. The pride of life
    4. Faith is the victory that overcomes the world

III. Conclusion
  A. *Rewards for Overcomers*
    (Rev. 2:11, 17, 26; 3:5, 12, 21)
  B. *A Call to Commitment for Those Who Long to Overcome*

Questions about Eternal Life

1 John 5:11–13

I. **Introduction**
  A. *Life Is Short at Its Longest*
    1. The psalmist's conclusion: 70–80 years (Ps. 90:10)
    2. Our average life span is still in that range
  B. *Jesus Came to Offer Something Better*
    1. "Everlasting life" (John 3:16; 5:24)
    2. "Eternal life" (John 17:3)
  C. *Human Questions about Living Forever*

II. **Body**
  A. *Where Is Eternal Life Found (v. 11)?*
    1. The search for eternal life
      a. Preserving the body in hope of eternal life
      b. Freezing the body in hope of eternal life
      c. Good works to gain eternal life
      d. Going through religious rituals to gain eternal life
      e. All of the above fall short of the goal (Eph. 2:8–9)
    2. Eternal life is a gift from God
      a. "God has given to us eternal life"
      b. "The gift of God is eternal life" (Rom. 6:23)
    3. Eternal life is found in Jesus ("this life is in His Son")
      a. Jesus purchased eternal life for us on the cross
      b. Jesus guaranteed eternal life by His resurrection
  B. *When Does Eternal Life Begin (v. 12)?*
    1. "He that hath the Son hath life"
      a. Eternal life begins when we have the Son
      b. Eternal life is then an immediate possession
    2. We do not wait until death to receive eternal life
    3. How do we get the Son?
      a. We receive Him by faith (John 1:12)
      b. Upon receiving Christ, we are justified (Rom. 5:1)
      c. At that moment we have peace with God (Rom. 5:1)

      d. At that moment we are born again
        (1 Peter 1:23)
      e. At that moment we receive eternal life
        (John 5:24)
    4. To reject Christ is to refuse eternal life
      a. "He that hath not the Son of God hath not life"
      b. Receive Christ and have eternal life now
  C. *How Can One Have Assurance of Eternal Life (v. 13)?*
    1. This was the purpose of John's epistle
      a. "That ye may know that ye have eternal life"
      b. John wanted God's children to be sure
    2. John stresses the present possession again
    3. Assurance comes from believing promises of
       eternal life
      a. Believe that God keeps His Word
      b. Rest on His promise of eternal life

III. Conclusion
  A. *Are You Sure That You Have Eternal Life?*
  B. *Make Sure by Coming in Faith to Christ Today*

From Sincerity to Certainty

Acts 10:43

I. Introduction
   A. *The Value of Sincerity*
      1. The opposite of hypocrisy
      2. Most respect sincere people
   B. *The Shortcomings of Sincerity*
      1. One can be sincerely wrong
      2. Sincere people have made tragic mistakes
      3. Sincerity in error does not save
   C. *Cornelius Becomes Certain of Salvation*
      1. Cornelius had been sincere but lost
      2. Peter was sent by the Lord to instruct him
      3. How Cornelius became saved and sure

II. Body
   A. *The Certainty of the Word (v. 43)*
      1. "To him give all the prophets witness"
      2. Cornelius had been devout
         a. He feared God, as did his family
         b. He was generous, giving alms
         c. He prayed without ceasing
      3. His sincerity was not enough to save him
      4. An angel told him to send for Peter (vv. 2–8)
      5. Peter instructed Cornelius in the Scriptures (v. 43)
   B. *The Certainty of the Whosoever (v. 43)*
      1. "That . . . whosoever believeth in him"
         a. No restrictions on who can be saved
         b. Christ died for us all
      2. This was new truth to Peter
         a. He had limited the Gospel to the Jews
         b. Now he had learned this good news was for everyone
      3. Peter had struggled with the "whosoever" question
         a. God opened Peter's eyes through a vision (vv. 9–16)
         b. Then messengers from Cornelius arrived
         c. Peter traveled with them to minister to Cornelius
      4. How grateful we can be that all can be saved!

    C. *The Certainty of the Washing Away of Sin (v. 43)*
      1. "... shall receive remission of sins"
      2. What good news!
        a. The sins of the past can be gone at last
        b. Complete forgiveness through faith alone
      3. Cornelius could be saved and certain
      4. We can be saved and certain too
        a. No more wondering if we've been good enough
        b. No more guilt over past sins
      5. We can simply believe and be saved (Acts 16:31)

III. **Conclusion**
    A. *Proof That All Can Be Saved (vv. 44–46)*
    B. *Baptism for These Who Were Certain of Salvation (vv. 47–48)*
    C. *How Certain Are You?*

Communion—Until He Comes

1 Corinthians 11:23–26

I. **Introduction**
   A. *The Christ Who Died and Rose Again Will Come Again*
      1. The promise of Jesus (John 14:1–3)
      2. The promise of angels (Acts 1:11)
      3. The promise of prophets and apostles (1 Thess. 4:13–18)
   B. *We Live in the Light of His Return*
   C. *What Does This Have to Do with Communion?*

II. **Body**
   A. *Christians Are to Meet for Communion Until He Comes (vv. 23–26)*
      1. Jesus instituted communion to commemorate His death
      2. Through the centuries, Christians have kept this appointment
      3. Why do Christians continue communion?
         a. To remember His death
         b. To rededicate their lives
         c. To forgive one another
         d. To obey regardless of the conditions
      4. What does communion mean to you?
      5. Has communion become only a faithless form?
      6. Each communion, expect Jesus to return
   B. *The Message of the Cross Will Endure Until He Comes (v. 26)*
      1. Times may change but not the message
         a. The Gospel is unchanged
         b. All sinners still need salvation
         c. Salvation was purchased at the cross
      2. The blood of Christ and O.T. sacrifices
         a. "Behold the Lamb of God" (John 1:29)
         b. No remission of sins without the blood (Heb. 9:22)
      3. Money cannot buy salvation (1 Peter 1:18–20)
         a. Not with corruptible things
         b. Not with silver and gold

    4. The cross is the theme of heaven's song
       (Rev. 1:5–7)
    5. The cross outlives its critics (1 Cor. 1:18)

C. *The Power of the Cross Will Change Lives Until He*
    Comes (v. 26)
    1. "The power of God unto salvation" (Rom. 1:16)
    2. The blood of Christ cleanses from all sin
       (1 John 1:7)
    3. Communion will always be relevant
       a. We need to remember Christ's death
       b. We need to keep the cross and His coming in
          mind
       c. These two give incentive and power for holy
          living
    4. Remembering His death is more than taking
       elements
       a. It is celebrating His love
       b. It is giving thanks for His grace
       c. It is praising God for His sacrifice
       d. It is rejoicing in salvation

III. Conclusion
    A. *Communion Is for Those Who Have Been Born Again*
    B. *Communion Is a Time for Making Things Right with*
       God and Other People
    C. *Are You Ready for Communion?*

Clean Feet

I. **Introduction**
   A. *The Hour of the Ages Had Arrived (v. 1)*
      1. It was time for Jesus to depart out of the world
      2. This was the time for which He was born
   B. *The Wickedness of Humanity Reached Its Climax (v. 2)*
      1. The plot for the betrayal of Jesus was under way
      2. Judas had decided to sell the Savior
   C. *Then Jesus Washed Their Feet*

II. **Body**
   A. *The Savior as a Servant (vv. 3–5)*
      1. He laid aside His garments
      2. See how this fit the pattern of Christ's work
         a. His position with His Father (v. 3)
         b. His leaving of heaven (rising from the table)
         c. His heavenly position laid aside (garments laid aside)
         d. His position as a servant (He took the towel)
      3. Jesus is still washing people (1 Cor. 6:9–11)
      4. The water and the washing
         a. Water symbolizes the Word of God (Eph. 5:25–27)
         b. His Word keeps us clean day by day
   B. *Peter and His Protest (vv. 6–11)*
      1. "Thou shalt never wash my feet"
      2. Peter thinks he can clean up his own life
         a. This is a hopeless task
         b. Peter will soon learn how hopeless
         c. Peter's coming boasts and denials
      3. "If I wash thee not, thou hast no part in me"
         a. Reformation does not save
         b. Only Christ can cleanse from sin
      4. Peter's cry for total cleansing (v. 9)
      5. Peter didn't need a bath; only his feet were dirty
      6. We are washed at salvation (Titus 3:5)
      7. Our feet get dirty walking in this dusty world

    C. *The Call to All Christians (vv. 12–17)*
1. "Ye ought to wash one another's feet"
2. What Jesus was saying:
   a. You ought to forgive
   b. You ought to be humble
   c. You ought to carefully apply the Bible to others
3. Are you like Jesus with His basin of water?
4. Do you help others keep their feet clean?

III. Conclusion
    A. *A Call to Humble Service*
    B. *A Call to a Clean Walk*
    C. *Only Jesus Can Keep Us Clean*

On to Jerusalem

Palm Sunday   *Luke 19:28–44*

I. **Introduction**
   A. *The Parable of the Returning King (vv. 12–27)*
      1. A nobleman who became a king
      2. A king who was rejected
      3. The return of the king
      4. A parable to prepare the disciples for what was ahead
   B. *Now It Was Time to Go to Jerusalem*
      1. The triumphal entry was ahead (Palm Sunday)
      2. His betrayal and trial were ahead
      3. The cross and resurrection were ahead

II. **Body**
   A. *Jesus Ascended to Jerusalem Because It Was Time (vv. 28–35)*
      1. Our Lord was always on time
         a. "Mine hour is not yet come" (John 2:4)
         b. "My time is not yet come" (John 7:6)
      2. Now His time had arrived
      3. Daniel's amazing prophecy would be fulfilled (Dan. 9:25)
      4. Note the timing of events that day
         a. The colt was there for the disciples to find (v. 32)
         b. The owners were there to react as prophesied (v. 33)
      5. God's great plan of redemption was right on schedule
      6. Dr. William Culbertson: "Calvary was not God's afterthought. It was His forethought."
      7. Jesus was coming into Jerusalem to die—right on time
   B. *Jesus Ascended to Jerusalem to Fulfill the Scriptures (vv. 36–40)*
      1. Zechariah saw it all centuries before (Zech. 9:9)
         a. The people would welcome Him with joy
         b. Shouts of praise would fill the air
         c. He would be riding an unbroken colt

55

    2. Jesus came to fulfill the Scriptures
      a. His birth in Bethlehem (Mic. 5:2)
      b. His virgin birth (Isa. 7:14)
      c. His rejection by men (Isa. 53:3)
      d. His substitutionary death (Isa. 53:5–6)
    3. This is the heart of the Gospel (1 Cor. 15:3–4)
      a. Our Lord is all He said He was
      b. The Scriptures guarantee Him
C. *Jesus Ascended to Jerusalem to Die for Sinners*
    (vv. 41–44)
    1. The love of Jesus brought Him to this earth
    2. The love of Jesus brought Him to Jerusalem
      a. His arrival would motivate His enemies
      b. His arrival would lead to the cross
    3. See His compassion for those who would crucify
      Him
      a. "He beheld the city, and wept over it" (v. 41)
      b. He mourned for their coming sorrows
        (vv. 42–44)
      c. He wept because they had missed their time
        (v. 44)

III. Conclusion
    A. *The People Missed Their Day of Visitation*
    B. *Don't Miss Your Greatest Opportunity*
    C. *Come in Faith to Jesus While You Have Time*

No Fault Found in Jesus

I. **Introduction**
   A. *From the Hosannas of Palm Sunday to Pilate's Hall*
      1. The betrayal by Judas
      2. Peter denies his Lord
      3. Jesus on trial
   B. *Christ Before Pilate*
      1. The earthly judge and the Judge of all the earth
      2. H. A. Ironside: "Pilate before Christ."
   C. *Pilate's Decision: "I Find in Him No Fault at All"*
      (v. 38)

II. **Body**
   A. *Here Is the Statement of a Firsthand Witness*
      1. Pilate was there
         a. Let today's critics of Christ be silenced
         b. Pilate's testimony would stand in any court
         c. He had personally examined the accused
      2. Pilate repeated his decision three times:
         (See 19:4, 6)
      3. Pilate's decision agrees with Scripture
         a. "Who did no sin" (1 Peter 2:22)
         b. "Holy, harmless, undefiled" (Heb. 7:26)
   B. *Here Is the Statement of One Who Was Searching for*
      Faults
      1. Pilate had frequent problems with the Jews
         a. They kept reporting him to Rome
         b. He was in trouble with Rome because of them
      2. He had been sent to Jerusalem to keep peace
         a. It was time for the Passover
         b. No riots wanted
      3. Pilate would like to have found a fault in Jesus
         a. He was searching for a fault
         b. He wanted to keep peace with the Jews
      4. Some people are always looking for faults
         a. Give them sunshine and they will worry about
            rain
         b. They are only happy when complaining
         c. They continually major on minors

57

       5. But Mr. Negative could find nothing wrong with our Lord

  C. *Here Is a Statement by One Who Rejected the Faultless One*

      1. Pilate found no fault in Jesus

        a. Neither did he place faith in Him

        b. His nice negative comment left him lost

      2. Pilate's moving question: "What shall I do then with Jesus which is called Christ?" (Matt. 27:22)

        a. He left life's greatest question to others

        b. He tried to be neutral; washed his hands (27:24)

        c. He claimed to be innocent (27:24)

        d. He decided by not deciding

III. Conclusion

  A. *What Will You Do with the Faultless One?*

  B. *Don't Make Pilate's Mistake*

  C. *Receive This Perfect Savior by Faith*

      1. Make life's greatest decision

      2. Believe and be saved (Acts 16:31)

The Crown of Thorns

Matthew 27:27–29

I. **Introduction**
   A. *What a Decision Pilate Had to Make!*
      1. He had to judge the Judge of all the earth
      2. He had to decide between Christ and the crowd
      3. We must each do the same
   B. *Pilate Offered the Crowd Jesus or Barabbas*
      1. The Master or the murderer
      2. Jesus took Barabbas' place. . . and yours and mine
   C. *The Whipping, the Mocking, the Crown of Thorns*

II. **Body**
   A. *They Placed a Crown upon Jesus but Did Not Make Him Their King*
      1. The soldiers dressed Jesus as a king
         a. The scarlet robe
         b. The crown of thorns
         c. They were only pretending
      2. Many pretend that Jesus is their king
         a. He seems to be king at church, but not at home
         b. He seems to be king before believers, but not at work
      3. The crown of thorns hurt Jesus, brought blood from His brow
         a. When we only pretend we hurt our Lord
         b. Let's really make Him king of our lives
   B. *They Praised Jesus but Did Not Mean What They Said*
      1. "Hail, King of the Jews"
         a. These were words of praise
         b. But they were mocking words
      2. Many say things about Jesus they do not mean
         a. Many songs are but lies
         b. Many commitments are never carried out
         c. Many testimonies don't ring true
      3. Jesus deserves our total dedication
      4. Let's give Him our lives without reservation

    C. *They Knelt as If to Worship Jesus but It Was All Form*
       1. How deeply His heart must have been grieved!
       2. In bowing they were just going through empty
          motions
          a. They hit Him with a reed
          b. They spat upon Him
          c. They wounded Him and now pretended to
            worship Him
       3. So it is with many today
          a. Too many theatrics
          b. Too little theology
       4. Jesus deserves worship from our hearts; nothing
          less

III. Conclusion
    A. *The Challenges before Us*
       1. To give the Lord control of our lives
       2. To praise the Lord from the depths of our hearts
       3. To worship the Lord in Spirit and in truth
    B. *Let the World Know He Is Really Our Savior and King*

Gambling for the Garments of Christ

Series on the Cross   *Matthew 27:35*

I. **Introduction**
   A. *The Cross: Where God Did His Best and Man Did His Worst*
      1. Christ and His compassion; man and his coarseness
      2. Christ and His righteousness; man and his rebellion
      3. Christ and His love; man and his lawlessness
   B. *Soldiers Gambling at the Cross*
      1. Above them Christ was paying sin's debt
      2. Looking down, they gambled for His garments

II. **Body**
   A. *They Were Reckless with Redemption*
      1. They were near Jesus, but far from Him
         a. Could have touched Him, but ignored Him
         b. Could have trusted Him, but treated Him shamefully
      2. They knew the facts but ignored their implications
      3. There will always be those who are reckless with redemption
         a. Who know about God's love but continue lost
         b. Who know about Christ's sacrifice but continue in sin
         c. Who know about God's Word but continue in wickedness
      4. Even these fulfill the Scriptures (Ps. 22:16)
   B. *They Were Occupied Only with Outward Things*
      1. They wanted the clothes of Christ, but not Him
         a. Glad to have His clothes but not His cross
         b. Glad to have His garments but not His grief
         c. Glad to have His robe but not His rejection
      2. Many occupied with things about Christ, but not with Him
         a. Rituals but not the Redeemer
         b. Legalism but not the Lord
         c. Religious work but not the Word
         d. Service but not the Savior

61

    3. They are close to the truth but miss it
    4. They are active in church but not alive in Christ
  C. *They Were Careless with the Clothes of Christ*
    1. God was man's first clothier
      a. Adam was clothed by God after the Fall (Gen. 3:21)
      b. The Second Adam was unclothed by sinful man at the cross
    2. Without Christ we are clothed in rags (Isa. 64:6)
    3. New clothes are provided to those who trust in Christ (Isa. 61:10)
      a. The garments of salvation
      b. A robe of righteousness

III. Conclusion
  A. *Don't Gamble with Eternal Issues*
    1. Without Jesus, you can't win
    2. Trusting Him, you can't lose
  B. *Faith in Christ Makes Heaven Sure*
    1. Face up to your sins
    2. Receive Christ by faith and be sure of heaven

Christ's Most Remarkable Convert

Series on the Cross   *Luke 23:32–43*

I. **Introduction**
    A. *Difficult to Choose the Most Remarkable Convert*
        1. Converts among the rich: Joseph of Aramathea
        2. Converts among the religious: Nicodemas
        3. Converts among the rejected: the woman at the well
    B. *The Most Remarkable May Be the Thief on the Cross*
        1. The paths of three men meeting in death
        2. Two were completely guilty; one completely innocent
        3. Two paying their debts to society; one our debt of sin
        4. One dying in sin, one dying to sin, one dying for sinners
    C. *What Makes This Conversion So Remarkable?*

II. **Body**
    A. *A Remarkable Prophecy (v. 32)*
        1. Jesus died between two criminals
        2. Jesus was to make His grave with the wicked (Isa. 53:9)
        3. He would die between them and His grave would be near them
        4. The "rich" must also be considered
            a. Joseph of Aramathea would place Jesus in his grave
            b. Joseph was a wealthy man
        5. All prophecies concerning Jesus must be fulfilled
        6. Many prophecies converged at the cross
    B. *A Remarkable Prayer (v. 42)*
        1. This thief realizes he is a sinner (v. 41)
            a. He admits his guilt
            b. He sees justice in his punishment
            c. He proclaims the righteousness of Christ

    2. The content of his remarkable prayer
      a. Called Jesus "Lord"
        (1) Never saw a miracle by Jesus
        (2) Never heard a sermon by Jesus
      b. "Remember me when"
        (1) Didn't pray to escape the cross
        (2) Believed the Lord would establish His kingdom
      c. Looked at the Crucified and called Him his King
    3. J. C. Ryle: "If ever there was a soul hovering on the brink of hell, it was the soul of this thief. Some would have thought him too wicked a man to be saved; but it was not so."
  C. *A Remarkable Promise (v. 43)*
    1. "Today, shalt thou be with me in paradise"
    2. The only promise from the cross
    3. The questions answered in this promise
      a. Salvation by faith alone assured
      b. Heaven immediately follows the death of a believer

III. Conclusion
  A. *Lessons from This Remarkable Text for Christians*
    1. Never give up on sinners
    2. Seize every opportunity to witness for Christ
  B. *Lessons from This Remarkable Text for Unbelievers*
    1. Any sinner can be saved by faith in Christ
    2. Don't wait one more moment to believe

Go Tell the Good News

Series on the Resurrection   *Matthew 28:1–7*

I. **Introduction**
   A. *An Earthquake on Easter Morning (vv. 1–2)*
      1. Three women arrive at the tomb with spices
      2. They arrive just in time for an earthquake
   B. *The Stone Is Rolled Away by the Angel of the Lord*
      1. The angel sits on the stone
      2. Demonstrates victory over death and the grave
   C. *Urgent News for the Disciples*
      1. The angel's command: "Go quickly and tell"
      2. What is this urgent news?

II. **Body**
   A. *The Grave Is Empty (v. 6)*
      1. "He is not here"
         a. The women had come in unbelief
         b. They expected to find a body
         c. They found an empty tomb
      2. Consider their confusion
         a. The appearance of the angel (v. 3)
         b. The shaking soldiers (v. 4)
         c. Their human fears (v. 5)
      3. The earthshaking events leading up to this moment
         a. Jesus before Pilate
         b. The scourging, the mocking, the crucifixion
      4. Now the empty tomb: what next?
   B. *Christ Is Risen (v. 6)*
      1. "He is risen"
      2. The importance of this news (1 Cor. 15:17–19)
         a. Without the resurrection there would be no hope
         b. Without the resurrection there would be no salvation
      3. But Christ has risen
         a. All He said was true
         b. Salvation by faith is sure
   C. *Jesus Is Lord (v. 6)*
      1. "He is risen, as he said"

    2. The resurrection proved the deity of Christ
      a. The sign: "Destroy this temple"
        (John 2:19–21)
      b. The sign of the prophet, Jonah
        (Matt. 12:39–40)
    3. The resurrection fulfilled His promise
      (John 10:17–18)
    4. The angel called Him Lord (v. 6)

III. Conclusion
    A. *The Disciples Must Be Notified Immediately*
      1. They must meet with Jesus
      2. He will commission them to reach the world
    B. *Are We Telling the Good News?*
      1. The need is great and the message unchanged
      2. Let's get serious about bringing people to Christ

Tell Peter

Mark 16:7

I. **Introduction**
   A. *The Early Morning Walk to the Tomb (vv. 1–4)*
      1. Three women come bringing spices
      2. They come to do the work of undertakers
      3. They worry about moving the stone at the tomb
         a. Unbelief is fertile ground for worrying
         b. There was no need to worry
         c. When they arrived the stone was rolled away
   B. *Three Women Commissioned by an Angel (vv. 5–7)*
      1. They were to put away their fears: Christ was alive!
      2. They were to tell the disciples Christ had risen
      3. They were to be sure to tell Peter
   C. *Why Must Peter Be Told?*

II. **Body**
   A. *Peter Needed to Know He Was Not Forsaken (14:22–72)*
      1. Jesus had prepared His disciples for what was ahead
         a. The crucifixion (vv. 22–25)
         b. Persecution (v. 27)
         c. His resurrection (v. 28)
      2. Peter vowed never to be offended (vv. 29–32)
      3. Peter had broken that vow (vv. 53–72)
         a. He needed to know that Jesus still loved him
         b. He needed to know that Jesus had kept His vow (v. 28)
      4. To fail does not make one a lifelong failure
         a. God's love reaches out to those who have failed
         b. The cross and the resurrection guarantee that love
   B. *Peter Needed to Know He Had Been Forgiven (vv. 53–72)*
      1. He had followed Jesus from afar
      2. He had mingled with the enemies of the Lord
      3. He had warmed himself by the wrong fire

    4. He had denied his Lord three times
       a. Didn't want to be identified with Jesus
       b. Cursed and swore, while denying he knew Jesus
    5. Your sins can be forgiven too

  C. *Peter Needed to Know He Had a Future with Jesus (v. 72)*
    1. He was a broken man
    2. Peter had been broken before
       a. When his net had broken (Luke 6:6)
       b. When his pride was broken (Luke 6:8)
       c. When his partnership was broken (Luke 6:9–10)
    3. He had left all to follow Jesus (Luke 6:11)
    4. Now he felt disqualified
    5. Peter needed to know he still belonged to the Lord

III. **Conclusion**
  A. *What the Resurrection Meant to Peter (1 Peter 1:5–8)*
    1. He called the resurrection his "living hope"
    2. He now knew that God had not given up on him
  B. *What Does the Resurrection Mean to You?*

The Lord Is Risen Indeed

Series on the Resurrection   *Luke 24:34*

I. Introduction
   A. *The Most Important Question Ever Asked: Is Christ
      Risen?*
      1. If He did not rise, faith is worthless (1 Cor. 15:17)
      2. If He did not rise, there is no hope of heaven
          (15:18)
      3. "But now is Christ risen from the dead" (15:20)
   B. *Looking in on a Convinced Crowd*
      1. They had doubted His promise but now believed
      2. Some had visited the tomb and found it empty
      3. Others had met Jesus along the way
   C. *Their Conclusion: "The Lord Is Risen Indeed"*

II. Body
   A. *These Words Speak of the Lord*
      1. "The Lord is risen"
      2. Since He is risen they know He is the Lord
      3. Remember the past impressions of some of them
          a. Some thought He was a great man
          b. Some thought He was a prophet
          c. Some thought He would deliver them from
              Rome's power
      4. Now they know they had underestimated Him
      5. The resurrection sets Christ apart from all others
   B. *These Words Speak of Life*
      1. "The Lord is risen indeed"
      2. So much of their past had spoken of death
          a. The betrayal and beating of Jesus
          b. The way of sorrows to the cross
          c. The crucifixion of Jesus
          d. The burial by Joseph and Nicodemas
      3. Doubts on the first Easter morning
          a. They were in despair over what had happened
          b. The women came to embalm His body
          c. They turned redemption into a ritual
      4. The resurrection changed everything
      5. The uniqueness of the Gospel is that it brings life

    C. *These Words Speak of Love*
      1. "And hath appeared to Simon"
      2. Jesus appeared to the man who had denied Him
        a. Cowardly Simon Peter
        b. Cursing Simon Peter
      3. The resurrection declares God's love for sinners
      4. The resurrection offers forgiveness to backsliders

III. Conclusion
    A. *The Living Lord Loves You*
    B. *The Cross Proves His Love*
    C. *The Resurrection Guarantees His Power to Save*

The Ever Living One

Series on the Resurrection   *Hebrews 7:25*

I. **Introduction**
   A. *Resurrection: the Scriptural Sign of the Deity of Christ*
      1. The temple destroyed and restored (John 2:18–22)
      2. Jonah three days in the whale (Matt. 12:38–40)
   B. *What Does the Resurrection Mean to You and Me?*
      1. Why is it important?
      2. What does it tell us about Jesus?

II. **Body**
   A. *He Is Able*
      1. "He is able to save to the uttermost"
         a. He is able to forgive our sins
         b. He is able to make us children of God
         c. He is able to be with us in trouble
         d. He is able to take us to heaven when we die
         e. He is able to raise us at His return
      2. How this was true during His earthly ministry
         a. Restoring life to the daughter of Jairus
            (Mark 5:22–43)
         b. Healing the woman who touched His garment
            (Mark 5:25–34)
         c. Raising Lazarus (John 11:38–46)
   B. *He Is Available*
      1. "All who come unto God by Him"
      2. Jesus always willing to let people get to Him
         a. He was available to children (Matt. 19:13–15)
         b. He was available to blind Bartimaeus (Mark
            10:46–52)
         c. He was available to Zacchaeus (Luke 19:1–10)
      3. Jesus is available to you and me today
         a. Even if we have neglected Him
         b. Even if, in the past, we have rejected Him
      4. All who call will find Him available
         (Rom. 10:9, 13)
   C. *He Is Alive*
      1. "Seeing He ever liveth to make intercession for
         them"

71

    2. The finished and unfinished work of Christ
       a. His work of redemption was finished at the cross
       b. His work of intercession continues to this day
    3. Since He is alive we have assurance for the future
       a. We do not face temptations alone
       b. We do not face trials alone
       c. When we stumble, He is there to pick us up
       d. When we sin, He is there to intercede

III. Conclusion
   A. *The Savior Who Is Sufficient for Us All*
   B. *Will You Make Him Your Own?*

The Ascension of Jesus Christ

Series on the Resurrection   *Acts 1:1–11*

I. **Introduction**
   A. *Forty Days after the Resurrection*
      1. The number of full probation or ample demonstration
         a. Israel in the wilderness forty years
         b. Ninevah to be destroyed in forty days
         c. Christ fasted forty days before being tempted
      2. Many appearances of the risen Christ during the forty days
   B. *The Neglected Experience*
      1. The Ascension is another mountaintop experience
         a. The Sermon on the Mount
         b. The Mount of Transfiguration
         c. The Olivet discourses
         d. The beginning of the Triumphal Entry
      2. Come view the ascension of the risen Christ

II. **Body**
   A. *Christ Ascended to Prepare a Place (v. 2)*
      1. The peaceful promises of the Upper Room (John 14:2)
         a. Before associated with His death
         b. Now, as He ascends, the promises echo again
      2. The Creator preparing for us from then until now
      3. We think too little of that prepared place
      4. What does the hope of heaven mean to you?
   B. *Christ Ascended to Prepare His People (vv. 4–8)*
      1. The promise of the Father (John 14:16, 26)
         a. The coming of the Holy Spirit
         b. The Holy Spirit to indwell believers (John 14:17)
      2. What the coming of the Holy Spirit would do
         a. Provide power for witnessing (v. 8)
         b. Provide peace for the afflicted (John 14:27)
         c. Provide power to live Christlike lives (Gal. 5:22–23)

73

C. *Christ Ascended to Prepare for His Return (vv. 6–11)*
1. The question about the kingdom (v. 6)
    a. Man's curiosity about the time of Christ's return
    b. No one knows this sacred secret (v. 7; Matt. 24:36)
2. This same Jesus will return (v. 11)
3. What will happen when Jesus returns?
    a. The saved will be resurrected (1 Thess. 4:13–16)
    b. Living believers will be caught up (1 Thess. 4:17)
4. What is the ascended Christ doing now?
    a. He is preparing places for us (John 14:1–3)
    b. He is interceding for us (Heb. 7:25; 1 John 2:1)
    c. He is moving people and nations into His prophetic plan
5. Christ will return right on time.

III. **Conclusion**
A. *Christ Prepared His Disciples for What Was Coming*
B. *Are You Prepared to Serve the Lord Until He Comes?*
C. *Are You Ready for Christ's Return?*

The Text for Us All

John 3:16

I. Introduction
   A. *The Most Familiar Verse in the Bible*
      1. Taught to children in Sunday school
      2. Whispered to loved ones on death beds
      3. Appears in crowds at athletic events
      4. Known by more people than any other Bible verse
   B. *Why John 3:16 Is a Text for Us All*
      1. Contains love enough for us all
      2. Contains sacrifice enough for us all
      3. Contains invitation enough for us all
      4. Contains life that is long enough for us all
   C. *Rediscovering John 3:16*

II. Body
   A. *Love Enough for Us All*
      1. "For God so loved the world"
      2. What if God had not loved the world
         a. We would all be without hope
         b. There would be no purpose in living
      3. God so loves us all
         a. No matter what we have done
         b. No matter what our positions in life
         c. No matter how worthless we feel
   B. *Sacrifice Enough for Us All*
      1. "That he gave his only begotten Son"
         a. The birth in Bethlehem is in these words
         b. The sinless life of Jesus is in these words
         c. The death of Jesus is in these words
         d. The resurrection of Jesus is in these words
      2. God's love moved Him to give His Son
      3. The sufficient sacrifice for our sins
         a. The Lamb of God sacrificed for us all (John 1:19)
         b. Cleansed from all sin (1 John 1:7–9)
         c. All our sins were laid on Him (Isa. 53:5–6)
         d. Washed from all our sins by His blood (Rev. 1:5)

C. *Invitation Enough for Us All*
1. "That whosoever believeth in Him"
2. *Whosoever* is a word for us all
   a. A word that is general, yet particular
   b. A word that embraces all, yet touches each one
3. Write your name in this text and believe

D. *Life That Is Long Enough for Us All*
1. "Should not perish, but have everlasting life"
2. Our natural life span is about 70–80 years
3. Everlasting life is far better

III. Conclusion

A. *Here, Then, Is a Message for Us All*
B. *How Will We Respond to It?*
C. *All Who Respond in Faith Receive Everlasting Life*

Head for the Hills

Psalm 121

I. Introduction
   A. *A Psalm for Those Who Need Help*
      1. If you need help this psalm is for you
      2. There is no other requirement for readers of this psalm
   B. *We All Often Need Help*
      1. In this world we have trouble (John 16:33)
      2. Sometimes people give us trouble
      3. Sometimes our bodies give us trouble
      4. Sometimes we bring trouble on ourselves
   C. *When Trouble Comes, Head for the Hills*

II. Body
   A. *Head for a Hill Called Sinai*
      1. Moses and Mt. Sinai (Ex. 20)
         a. Moses and the burning bush
         b. Moses called to deliver his people
         c. Moses bringing plagues upon Pharaoh
         d. Moses leading Israel through the Red Sea
         e. Moses on the mount with God
      2. On Mt. Sinai, Moses received the Law of God
         a. The law that declared God's holiness
         b. The law that sets down unchanging principles
      3. This holy, unchanging God offers help to those in distress
   B. *Head for a Hill Called Calvary*
      1. The place Jesus died to satisfy the law
         a. The place of mercy and grace
         b. Where God was just and the justifier (Rom. 3:23–26)
         c. Where forgiveness flows freely
      2. This is the hill of salvation and hope
         a. Are you burdened with sin?
         b. Do you long for assurance of heaven?
      3. The cross the cure
         a. When you are in pain
         b. When you are unwilling to forgive

   c. When you have been wounded by another
   d. When you are offended
  4. There's room at the cross for you
 C. *Head for a Hill Called Olivet*
  1. This is the place of the ascension of the living Christ
   a. Christ had risen as He said
   b. We serve a living Savior
  2. The disciples were commissioned here (Acts 1:8)
  3. The promise of His return was given by angels (Acts 1:11)
  4. He will someday return here to set up His kingdom

III. Conclusion
 A. *An Invitation to Those Who Need Help*
  1. Come in faith to this righteous Savior
  2. Come in faith to this crucified Savior
  3. Come in faith to this risen, returning Savior
 B. *You Will Find Grace to Help in Your Time of Need*

Peace, Be Still

Mark 4:35–41

I. Introduction
A. *Our Lord's Long Day of Preaching*
  1. The crowd so great He taught from a boat
  2. Topics for His teaching:
     a. The parable of the sower
     b. The candle under a bushel
     c. The coming harvest
     d. The mustard seed
B. *Jesus with His Disciples at Day's End*
  1. Closing the day with an adventure
  2. A time the disciples would never forget

II. Body
A. *The Promise at Evening (v. 35)*
  1. "Let us pass over to the other side"
  2. What a great promise!
     a. Speaks of a journey with Jesus
     b. Speaks of His fellowship on the other side
     c. Speaks of safe passage for the journey
  3. The Christian life is like this journey
     a. We may be weary when He calls us
     b. We decide to travel with Him
     c. He goes with us the entire journey
     d. We are guaranteed safe passage to heaven
  4. Be sure you are traveling with Jesus
B. *The Peril Brought by the Storm (v. 37)*
  1. "There arose a great storm of wind"
  2. The waves started coming into the ship
  3. How devastating the upheavals of nature!
     a. It has not always been so: Eden's tranquility
     b. There is a better day ahead (Isa. 35)
  4. Lessons for the disciples in the storm
     a. They were obeying, yet the storm came
     b. They were traveling with Jesus, yet the storm came
     c. They were in the center of His will, yet the storm came
  5. Storms come to us all

C. *The Purpose of the Storm (vv. 38–41)*
1. Jesus knew the storm would come
2. He was equipped to send the storm away
3. He chose to go through the storm with His disciples
4. The storm enabled them to measure their faith
   a. They learned that Christ is with us in storms
   b. They learned that He is up to any occasion
5. Different storms for different purposes
   a. Jonah's storm was to bring him back to the Lord
   b. Paul's storm was to provide witnessing opportunities
   c. This storm was to build the disciples' faith
6. Don't judge the purpose of another's storm

III. Conclusion
A. *Jesus and His "Peace, Be Still"*
B. *What Manner of Man Is This?*
1. He is one who invites us to travel with Him
2. He is one who goes with us through our storms
3. He is one who is always up to the occasion

God's Great Woman

I. **Introduction**
  A. *Elisha and the Great Woman at Shunem (v. 8)*
    1. God is careful with His adjectives
    2. This must have been an unusual woman
  B. *What Made the Shunamite Woman Great?*
    1. What qualities of character made her unusual?
    2. What can mothers learn from her?

II. **Body**
  A. *Her Compassion for the Prophet of God (vv. 9–10)*
    1. Elisha evidently often traveled to Shunem
      a. He was acquainted with this family
      b. When he came to Shunem he stopped there to eat
    2. This great woman saw Elisha's need for lodging
      a. She recognized him as a man of God
      b. She urged her husband to add a room for Elisha
    3. She cared enough to get involved
      a. She designed and furnished a room for Elisha
      b. She extended a standing invitation to him
    4. Great mothers are people of compassion
  B. *Her Contentment with the Provision of God (vv. 12–17)*
    1. Elisha wanted to do something to repay this woman
      a. "What is to be done for thee?"
      b. Elisha offered to speak to influential people for her
    2. This great woman turned down the prophet's offer
      a. "I dwell with mine own people"
      b. She is content with what she has (1 Tim. 6:6)
    3. Elisha promised her a son
      a. He concluded this was her desire
      b. He promised a child within a year
      c. The child was born as promised
    4. God honored her contentment
      a. She didn't complain
      b. God gave her the desire of her heart

  C. *Her Confidence in the Power of God (vv. 18–37)*
   1. The child became ill and died
    a. He had joined his father among the reapers
    b. A severe headache sent him to his mother
    c. The child died on his mother's lap
   2. The great woman's confidence in a crisis
    a. She sends for Elisha and trusts the Lord
    b. "It shall be well" (v. 23)
    c. "It is well" (v. 26)
   3. She knew that God would care for the child
    a. Even death did not destroy her faith
    b. Elisha's hurried trip to Shunem to heal her son
   4. The child lives by the power of God (vv. 32–37)

III. **Conclusion**
  A. *A Mother's Faith Rewarded*
   1. God answered this mother's prayers
   2. He has answered the prayers of many mothers
  B. *Is Your Mother Praying for You?*

What Aileth Thee, Hagar?

Mother's Day   *Genesis 21:17*

I. **Introduction**
   A. *Hagar: The Mother of the Arab Nations*
      1. Well known that Abraham is the father of Israel
      2. He is also the father of the Arab nations (Gen. 16)
      3. Sarah is the mother of Israel
      4. Hagar is the mother of the Arab nations
   B. *The Birth of Ishmael (Gen. 16)*
      1. God's original promise to Abraham (Gen. 15:4–6)
      2. Sarah's plan: Hagar to provide Abraham a son
   C. *Isaac's Birth and Hagar's Heartache (Gen. 21)*
      1. Hagar and Ishmael cast out into the desert
      2. Hagar's cry and God's question: What aileth thee, Hagar?

II. **Body**
   A. *God's Question When a Mother Was Grieving for Her Child*
      1. Hagar thought her child would die
      2. Mothers have shed many tears over their children
         a. In times of sickness
         b. When children have been wayward
         c. When they have been in danger
      3. Mothers have
         a. Hidden their tears when harsh words were spoken
         b. Prayed through their tears when wounded and broken
         c. Waited long years by their children neglected
         d. Cried to the God whom their children rejected
      4. But in that hour God cared about Hagar's tears
      5. He called upon Hagar to unburden her heart
   B. *God's Question to a Mother Who Had Been Wronged by Others*
      1. She had been wronged by man
      2. She had been wronged by a man of God
         a. She had seen him at prayer
         b. She had admired his courage and faith

83

   3. She had known him in his greatest weakness
   4. Sarah had taken part in this wrong
   5. We are not always what we should be
   6. Have you been wounded by a professing
       Christian?
C. *God's Question to a Mother Who Was to Learn of His
    Faithfulness*
   1. She had started this journey with bread and water
   2. Now her bread was eaten and her water gone
   3. What God did not advise Hagar to do:
       a. Grieve over her problems
       b. Hold grudges and nurse her wounds
   4. Instead He opened her eyes to His provision
       a. There was water within reach
       b. God has provided for all of our needs

III. Conclusion

A. *Hagar's Response: She Filled the Bottle and Gave
    Water to Ishmael*
   1. Water to sustain life was available to this troubled
       mother
   2. God has provided living water to give eternal life
   3. This living water is ours through faith in Christ
B. *What Will You Do with the Blessing of Eternal Life
    Provided to You?*
   1. Will you share the living water?
   2. Will you tell others of Christ and His love?

Be Strong

Ephesians 6:10

I. Introduction
   A. *A Command from Paul for Us All: Be Strong!*
      1. We need to be strong because of our adversaries
      2. We need to be strong because of our testimonies
   B. Finally—*A Word That Looks Backward and Forward*
      1. Looks back to the rich truths of this epistle
      2. Looks ahead to the conflicts of the Christian life
   C. *Considering These Important Words: Be Strong!*

II. Body
   A. *Be Strong! These Are Military Words*
      1. Every believer is enlisted in a battle
      2. Paul is about to reveal the Enemy (vv. 11–12)
         a. We face a powerful enemy with many allies
         b. We must be strong for the battle
      3. In what areas do we need to be strong?
         a. Strong in character (v. 14)
         b. Strong in faith (v. 16)
         c. Strong in Bible knowledge (v. 17)
         d. Strong in prayer (v. 18)
   B. *Be Strong! These Can Be Mocking Words*
      1. Sometimes good words are meaningless
      2. Perhaps these good words mock you today
         a. You feel especially weak
         b. Your trials have you on the ropes
         c. Temptation has edged you to a precipice
         d. You wonder if you can go on
      3. You've tried to be strong
         a. Intended to clean up your language
         b. Tried to control your temper
         c. Made an effort to stop worrying
         d. Resolved to stop wounding with your tongue
         e. Decided to maintain a devotional life
      4. You keep failing over and over again
   C. *Be Strong! The Words That Follow Make These Miraculous Words*
      1. "Be strong in the Lord and in the power of His might"

    2. Some battles are too tough for us
    3. Some adversaries are too strong for us
    4. We have a powerful Savior (Matt. 28:18)
      a. This changes the picture
      b. We can exchange our weakness for His strength (Isa. 40:31)
      b. We can do all things through Christ (Phil. 4:13)

III. Conclusion
    A. *Our Crucified and Living Lord Gives the Victory*
      1. He invites all defeated ones to come to Him
      2. Trusting Him we are sure to overcome
    B. *Faith Overcomes the World (1 John 5:4)*

Onward Christian Soldiers

Ephesians 6:12–18

I. **Introduction**
  A. *The Christian Life Is the Beginning of Many Things*
    1. Fellowship, hope, joy, assurance of heaven
    2. The beginning of a fight with unseen enemies
  B. *J. C. Ryle on the Fight:*
    "It is a fight of perpetual necessity. It admits of no breathing time, no armistice, no truce. On week-days as well as on Sundays—in private as well as in public—at home by the family fireside as well as abroad.
  C. *We Are Equipped to Win*

II. **Body**
  A. *The Armor of Consistency (vv. 14–15)*
    1. Our loins girt about with truth
      a. This was to prevent tangling and falling
      b. Calls for truthfulness; our Enemy a liar (John 8:44)
    2. The breastplate of righteousness
      a. Imputed righteousness by faith (Rom. 4:4)
      b. Imparted righteousness (Rom. 8:4)
      c. Righteousness as demonstrated in our lives
      d. This armor protects the heart
      e. We are soon defeated if we do not live right
    3. Our feet shod with the preparation of the gospel of peace
      a. Living the Gospel so others will find Christ
      b. Speaking the Gospel to those who are lost
      c. Taking the Gospel to those who have not heard
    4. We are called to practice what we preach
  B. *The Armor of Confidence (vv. 16–17)*
    1. The shield of faith: confidence in Christ
      a. Protection from the missiles of the Enemy
      b. We must believe our beliefs and doubt our doubts

       c. The Christian life begins and continues in faith
   2. The helmet of salvation
       a. Why the head and not the heart
       b. The importance of "know-so" salvation
       c. Assurance assures victory
  C. *The Armor of Communication (vv. 17–19)*
   1. The sword of the Spirit: the Word of God
       a. God communes with us through the Bible
       b. We must get our marching orders each day
       c. Neglect of the Bible brings defeat
   2. Praying always
       a. We commune with God through prayer
       b. "Pray without ceasing" (1 Thess. 5:17)
       c. Praying in the Spirit
       d. Praying for fellow soldiers (vv. 18–19)

III. Conclusion
  A. *Our Armor Protects Us as We Advance*
  B. *Our Lord Will Never Sound Retreat*
  C. *Expect to Win Each Encounter Every Day*

Jesus at a Grave

Memorial Day   *John 11:38*

I. Introduction
  A. *A Day to Remember*
    1. Remembering those who have died to preserve freedom
    2. Remembering loved ones who have died
    3. Decorating graves and remembering
  B. *What Jesus Did at a Grave*
    1. He wept and groaned within
    2. What this verse tells us about Jesus

II. Body
  A. *Jesus Understands Our Grief*
    1. Lazarus had been a good friend
    2. Jesus had come to resurrect him
    3. Still, He wept with those who grieved their loss
      a. He understood Mary's broken heart
      b. He understood Martha's tears
      c. He understood the pain of separation
    4. The promises: everlasting life, heaven, resurrection
    5. Nevertheless, it is normal to grieve when loved ones die
      a. Tears are God's safety valve for our emotional health
      b. Jesus understood this; He groaned and wept
  B. *Jesus Enters into Our Pain*
    1. Some understand but do nothing to help
    2. Jesus enters into our pain and ministers to us
      a. He saw the pain of a blind man and gave him sight
      b. He saw the pain of a lame man and made him walk
      c. He saw the pain of 10 lepers and restored their health
    3. Jesus is here today entering into your grief
    4. The cross proves His love
      a. Dying to pay for our sins
      b. Assuring paradise to a dying thief
    5. Bring your sorrow to the One who cares

    C. *Jesus Offers Hope to Those Who Are Hurting*
       1. The tender Savior is always triumphant
          a. He died and rose again
          b. He was victorious over the grave
       2. Jesus was up to the occasion
          a. "Take ye away the stone" (v. 39)
          b. "Lazarus, come forth" (v. 43)
          c. Lazarus came forth alive
       3. Jesus will bring hope to you
          a. On the darkest day, He makes a way
          b. Bring your broken heart to Him

III. Conclusion
    A. *Have Memories Brought You Down?*
    B. *Make This a Memorable Day*
       1. Allow the Lord to minister to your grief
       2. Trust the One who really cares

Memorials to the Master

Memorial Day

1 Corinthians 11:23;
Romans 6:3–4; 1 Peter 2:21

I. Introduction

  A. *Celebrating Memorial Day*

    1. Officially a day to remember those fallen in battle

    2. The price of freedom has always been high

  B. *We Take Too Lightly the Blessings Bought with Blood*

  C. *The Death of Christ also Purchased Freedoms*

    1. Freedom from fear, death, hell

    2. Freedom from the slavery of sin

  D. *Let's Consider Some Memorials to the Master*

II. Body

  A. *The Lord's Supper (1 Cor. 11:23)*

    1. The Lord's Supper is a memorial to Christ's death

    2. Misunderstandings about the Lord's Table

      a. Some think of it as a means to salvation

      b. Some think it was only for the early church

      c. Some think it takes away sin

      d. Some think it offers up Christ's body again and again

    3. Communion is a memorial; a picture of Christ's death

    4. Learning from this memorial

      a. The seriousness of sin

      b. The greatness of God's love

      c. The cost of salvation

  B. *Baptism (Rom. 6:3–4)*

    1. Baptism is a memorial to Christ's burial and resurrection

    2. What baptism is

      a. Following Jesus (Matt. 3:13–17)

      b. Obeying Jesus (Matt. 28:18–20)

      c. Public identification with Jesus (Acts 2:41)

    3. Have you been baptized?

    4. How did you prepare your heart for baptism?

    5. Were you walking more closely with Jesus at that time?

    6. Is it time for a new dedication to the One who died for you?

   C. *A Christlike Life (1 Peter 2:21)*
     1. A Christlike life is a memorial to the lordship of Christ
     2. We are the only Bibles some will read
     3. Let every word and deed remind people of Jesus
     4. This declares the lordship of Christ in you
     5. Who rules your life?

III. Conclusion
   A. *What Kind of a Memorial to Christ Are You?*
   B. *Many Need to Be Free*
     1. The truth sets people free (John 8:32)
     2. The power of Christ sets people free (John 8:36)
   C. *Make This Memorial Day a Day to Remember*
     1. Come and receive the One who died for you
     2. Surrender completely to Him

God's Unfailing Success Formula

Graduation Sunday   *Proverbs 3:5–6*

I. Introduction

    A. *Everyone Wants to Be Successful*

       1. The stress on education for success

       2. Hopes of parents for successful children

       3. Dreams of youth to be successful

    B. *What Is Success?*

       1. It is not financial security (Mark 8:36)

       2. Fame and popularity are both fleeting (1 John 2:17)

       3. Success is living in the will of God (1 John 2:17)

    C. *How to Have God's Direction in All We Do*

II. Body

    A. *Receive the Son of God*

       1. "Trust in the Lord with all thine heart"

       2. God's formula for success begins with faith

          a. Trust = faith or "believe"

          b. "Trust in the Lord" occurs 152 times in the Old Testament

          c. Equivalent to "Believe on the Lord Jesus Christ"

       3. Success begins with being born again (John 3:3–5)

          a. Nicodemas, though successful, needed salvation

          b. He was a religious ruler but was lost

          c. Begin at the beginning: receive Jesus now (John 1:12)

    B. *Read the Word of God*

       1. "Lean not to thine own understanding"

       2. Human understanding is limited and often faulty

          a. Our learning has not brought key answers to life

          b. Can be educated but miss the truth (2 Tim. 3:7)

       3. The Bible gives God's view of life

          a. It imparts wisdom (Ps. 119:99)

          b. It gives understanding (Ps. 119:104)

          c. It brings light (Ps. 119:130)

          d. It builds faith (Rom. 10:17)

       4. No success apart from applying God's Word to life

  C. *Recognize the Hand of God*
   1. "In all thy ways acknowledge him"
   2. God is at work in all events in our lives
    a. "All things are of God" (2 Cor. 5:18)
    b. "All things work together for good"
     (Rom. 8:28)
   3. See God's hand in everything
    a. This will remove anxiety and increase joy
    b. This will make you a positive praising person

III. Conclusion
  A. *Our Part in This Unfailing Success Formula*
   1. We must begin with faith
   2. We must make choices in faith
   3. We must dare to take steps of faith
  B. *God's Part: "He Shall Direct Thy Paths"*
   1. This is successful living
    a. Knowing God's will and doing it
    b. Having the leading of God every day
   2. God will come through!
   3. Will you?

The High Cost of Being Lost

Luke 12:16–21

I. **Introduction**
   A. *The Cost of Being Lost a Neglected Subject*
      1. Most preaching has to do with happy themes
         a. The blessings of the Christian life
         b. The prospect of the joys of heaven
      2. Truth demands balance
         a. We must face the cost of being lost
         b. We must warn the lost to escape hell
   B. *A Sad Parable of a Lost Man Who Lost Everything*
      1. He is prosperous but pitiful
      2. He is rich but ends his life in regret
   C. *Why the Rich Fool Lost It All*

II. **Body**
   A. *His Happiness Was Limited to the Happenings of Earth (v. 16)*
      1. "The ground of a certain rich man brought forth plentifully"
         a. Everything seemed to be going so well
         b. Success in farming made him happy
      2. Investments here are always risky
      3. What financial reverses would have done to him
         a. A drought would have devastated him
         b. Too much rain would have ruined him
      4. He had no inner peace for adverse circumstances
      5. Only faith in Christ equips us for tough times (Rom. 8:38–39)
   B. *His Holdings Were Limited to the Harvests of Earth (vv. 17–18)*
      1. "What shall I do . . . ?"
      2. His prosperity produced problems
         a. He didn't know what to do with success
         b. His increasing wealth complicated his life
         c. He gave no thought to sharing with others
      3. The rich fool suffered from *I* trouble
         a. "This will I do: I will pull down my barns"

   b.   His new barns would advertise his affluence
   c.   "There will I bestow all my fruits and my
        goods"
4.   Everything this rich fool harvested was perishable
5.   Faith in Christ prevents perishing (John 3:16)
C.   *His Hopes Were Limited to the Horizons of Earth
     (vv. 19–20)*
   1.   The rich fool was prepared for retirement
        a.   He looked to the future with confidence
        b.   "Take thine ease, eat, drink, and be merry"
   2.   His plan for the future was faulty
        a.   He planned on ease, eating, and entertainment
        b.   He neglected to plan for eternity
        c.   That night he faced death, the grave, and hell
   3.   The rich fool would leave his riches behind
   4.   Others would own all he had worked so hard to
        gain
   5.   He would lose everything, including his soul

III.   **Conclusion**
   A.   *Many Are Like the Rich Fool (v. 21)*
      1.   They invest their lives in temporal trinkets
      2.   They could come to Christ and gain eternal
           treasures
   B.   *Real Riches Are Laid Up in Heaven by Those Who
        Trust in Jesus*
   C.   *How Rich Are You?*

God Wants to Make a Deal

Isaiah 41:10

I. **Introduction**
   A. *A Text That Anticipates Our Needs*
      1. Meets us in anxiety and brings assurance
      2. Moves us from fear to faith
   B. *What God Wants to Do for His Children*
      1. If you are a Christian, God wants you to be blessed
      2. He longs to exchange His peace for your pain

II. **Body**
   A. *God Wants to Trade His Fellowship for Your Fears*
      1. "Fear thou not; for I am with thee"
      2. Fear stalks us all
      3. The four basic fears:
         a. Fear of death
         b. Fear of failure
         c. Fear of losing security
         d. Fear of the future
      4. God answers all of these fears:
         a. Death: "to die is gain" (Phil. 1:21)
         b. Failure: "I can do all things" (Phil. 4:13)
         c. Security: "My God shall supply all your need" (Phil. 4:19)
         d. Future: "Lo, I am with you always" (Matt. 28:20)
      5. Our Lord will never leave nor forsake us (Heb. 13:5–6)
   B. *God Wants to Trade His Comfort for Your Confusion*
      1. "Be not dismayed; for I am thy God"
      2. Dismay: "Why did this happen to me?"
      3. Confusion: can't understand why God allows trials
      4. God owns us as His own, even in tough times
      5. Whatever happens, we belong to Him
   C. *God Wants to Trade His Strength for Your Weakness*
      1. "I will strengthen thee"
      2. So many reasons for feeling weak:
         a. Sickness
         b. Regrets over past failures
         c. Conflict with the tempter

    3. Consider His strength (Isa. 40:28–31)
       a. God never becomes weary, never feels faint
       b. He gives power to the faint
       c. He imparts strength to those He loves
  D. *God Wants to Trade His Help for Your Helplessness*
    1. "I will help thee"
    2. Sometimes all we can do is cry for help
    3. Reach out to Jesus, He's reaching out to you
  E. *God Wants to Trade His Righteousness for Your Rags*
    1. Our righteousness is like filthy rags (Isa. 64:6)
    2. Jesus has made righteousness available through faith
       a. He took our sins upon Himself
       b. We receive His righteousness by faith (2 Cor. 5:21)
    3. "The right hand of my righteousness"
       a. Christ the Son of His right hand (Acts 7:55; Heb. 10:12)
       b. He intercedes for us there (Heb. 7:25; 1 John 2:1)

III. Conclusion
  A. *Come and Exchange Your Problems for God's Solutions*
  B. *Christ Is Sufficient for All Your Needs*

Getting Ready to Die

2 Kings 20:1–7

I. **Introduction**
   A. *Death: The Subject We Avoid*
      1. Death insurance is called life insurance
      2. Cemeteries become memorial gardens
      3. Few sermons are given to preparing for death
   B. *The King Who Was Told to Get Ready to Die (v. 1)*
      1. King Hezekiah was sick and told he would die
         a. Isaiah told him to set his house in order
         b. The king was given no hope of living
      2. Lessons to learn from a dying king

II. **Body**
   A. *Death Is Coming to Us All (v. 1)*
      1. "It is appointed unto men once to die" (Heb. 9:27)
         a. Adam was never born, but died
         b. Methusalah lived 969 years, but died
         c. Samson was the strongest of men, but died
         d. Solomon was wiser than all, but died
      2. Death is the result of sin (Rom. 5:12–14)
      3. Jesus came to die to pay for our sins
         a. Though sinless, He paid the ultimate penalty for sin
         b. He died as the substitute for sinners (Isa. 53:5–6)
         c. His resurrection proves His victory over death
      4. Faith in Christ assures everlasting life (1 John 5:13)
   B. *We Are Not Prepared to Live Until Prepared to Die (v. 1)*
      1. "Set thine house in order"
      2. We ought to prepare for death
      3. We should set our business affairs in order
         a. Family members ought to be protected
         b. Loved ones should not be left with debts
         c. This brings peace of mind for us now and for them later

  4. We should also set our spiritual affairs in order
   a. We can prepare to meet God (Amos 4:12)
   b. We prepare by being born again (John 3:3–5)
  5. Faith in Christ prepares one both to live and to die
   a. Jesus makes life worth living (John 10:10)
   b. Jesus takes the sting out of dying
    (1 Cor. 15:55–57)
   c. Life then has purpose and death is gain
    (Phil. 1:21–23)
 C. *The Time of Death Is Determined by the Lord (vv. 2–7)*
  1. Hezekiah had been pronounced terminal
  2. Prayer changed the king's dying date
   a. He had already learned the value of prayer
    (19:14–18)
   b. God had delivered him from Sennacherib's
    army
   c. Now he prays for God to give him years to live
    (vv. 2–3)
  3. God's wonderful answer to Hezekiah's prayer
   (vv. 5–6)
   a. "I have heard thy prayer"
   b. "I have seen thy tears"
   c. "I will heal thee"
   d. "I will add unto thy days fifteen years"

III. Conclusion
 A. *Is Your House in Order?*
 B. *Are You Prepared for Life or Death?*
 C. *Have You Been Given Bad News?*
 D. *Pray and Believe: With God All Things Are Possible*

Meet Jairus—Great Father

Father's Day   *Luke 8:40–56*

I. **Introduction**
   A. *Men the World Regards as Great*
      1. Kings who have kept the peace or conquered territory
      2. Generals who have been great leaders in battle
      3. Athletes who have thrilled the spectators
   B. *The View from Above*
      1. Men who have come to faith in Christ
      2. Men who have been faithful to their wives
      3. Men who have been examples to their children
   C. *Why Jairus Should Be Regarded as a Great Father*

II. **Body**
   A. *Jairus Did the Greatest Thing a Father Can Do (v. 41)*
      1. He came to Jesus
      2. Who Jairus was
         a. A ruler in the synagogue
         b. A leader among his people
      3. How Jairus came
         a. He came humbly: fell at Jesus' feet
         b. He came with a troubled heart
      4. What brought Jairus to Jesus
         a. An upset in his home
         b. A problem he could not solve
         c. A need of the touch of God on one he loved
      5. The greatest thing anyone can do is come to Jesus
   B. *Jairus Demonstrated the Greatest Example of a Father's Love (v. 42)*
      1. He came to talk to Jesus about his child
      2. The most privileged children in the world
         a. Those whose parents pray for them
         b. Those whose names are often before the throne of grace
      3. The most underprivileged children
         a. Those who grow up in godless homes
         b. Those whose parents do not pray for them

    4. We can pray for our children and expect answers
    5. Bible examples of praying fathers: Noah, Abraham, Job, Joshua

  C. *Jairus Faced the Greatest Test of a Father's Faith (vv. 49–56)*
    1. When he awaits news of his child's welfare
    2. When the news came it was bad: his daughter was dead
    3. Encouragement from Jesus at this dark development
      a. "Fear not: believe only, and she shall be made whole"
      b. Nothing takes Jesus by surprise
    4. Jesus had prepared Jairus for this moment
      a. The healing of the woman along the way (vv. 41–48)
      b. Walking with Jesus we encounter faith builders

III. Conclusion

  A. *The Daughter of This Great Father Was Healed (vv. 51–56)*
    1. Healed by our great Savior
    2. Nothing is beyond His power

  B. *Fear Not, Believe Only, and See What Jesus Does for You*

Pleasing God

I. **Introduction**
   A. *What a Wonderful Desire: To Please God!*
      1. The desire of the heroes of the faith
      2. Should also be our desire
   B. *If You Desire to Please God You're in the Right Place*
   C. *A Study in Pleasing God*

II. **Body**
   A. *The Impossibility of Pleasing God without Faith*
      1. "But without faith it is impossible to please him"
      2. Basics in pleasing God prohibited without faith
         a. Salvation is by faith (Eph. 2:8–9; Rom. 5:1)
         b. Answered prayer is through faith (James 1:6–8)
      3. Religious activity does not always please God
         a. Faithless religious ceremonies do not please God
         b. Faithless giving does not please God
      4. This verse proves two great facts:
         a. It is possible to please God
         b. Faith is available to all (John 3:16)
      5. What is faith?
         a. It is the substance of things hoped for (11:1)
         b. It is the evidence of things not seen (11:1)
         c. It is believing God and accepting His invitation
   B. *The Ingredients of the Faith That Pleases God*
      1. We must believe that God exists
         a. One thing to pray, another to believe God hears
         b. One thing to worship, another to believe it's accepted
      2. We must believe God rewards those who diligently seek Him
      3. Faith that pleases God is more than profession (James 2:14)
      4. Real faith changes lives (2 Cor. 5:17)
      5. See how the lives of these people of faith were changed

      a. Faith made Abel worship God
      b. Faith made Enoch walk with God
      c. Faith made Noah work for God

  C. *The Invitation to Faith That Pleases God*
    1. "He that cometh to God must believe"
    2. An invitation in the middle of the verse
    3. God continually invites us to faith in Christ
    4. This invitation reminds us of John 6:37
      a. An invitation to come to Jesus
      b. Assurance that He receives all to come to Him

III. Conclusion
  A. *Here Is an Invitation to Eternal Life*
    1. An invitation apart from works
    2. An invitation apart from religious ceremony
    3. An invitation to come as you are to Jesus
  B. *Come in Faith and God Will Be Pleased to Accept You*
  C. *Our Loving Lord Will Not Turn One Away*

Home Sweet Home

Luke 8:39

I. **Introduction**
   A. *The Sad Story of a Demon-Possessed Man*
      1. A man who lived in a cemetery
      2. A man who was self-destructive (Mark 5:1–5)
      3. A man who was uncontrollable (Mark 5:1–5)
   B. *Jesus Demonstrated His Power over Satan*
      1. The man was set free from his tormentors
      2. He was calm and clothed and in his right mind
      3. The Lord sent him home to show what had happened to him
   C. *Why Jesus Sent the Delivered Man Home*

II. **Body**
   A. *Home Is the First Frontier of the Christian Faith*
      1. Noah won his family to the Lord (Gen. 6:7)
      2. Joshua: "As for me and my house" (Josh. 24:15)
      3. Cornelius gathered his family to hear Peter (Acts 10:24)
      4. The Philippian jailer and his family believed (Acts 16:34)
      5. Our families should be the first to know our faith is real
         a. It is most difficult to be Christlike at home
         b. At home our witness stands or falls
      6. How strong is your testimony at home?
   B. *Home Is the Place to Glory in the Good Things of God*
      1. "Show what great things the Lord hath done to thee"
      2. Do you major on your blessings at home?
         a. Do loved ones see you as a genuine Christian?
         b. Are you known at home for faith or for fault finding?
      3. Do you appear holy at church and hateful at home?
      4. Are you saintly at church and sour at home?
      5. Are you gracious at church and grouchy at home?

      6. Is your home a place of praise or of pouting?

      7. Do you glory in the goodness of God at home?

   C. *Home Is the Outpost for Outreach with the Gospel of Christ*

      1. This man started at home and spread the word

      2. He shared his testimony throughout the city

      3. Christian homes should be lighthouses

         a. Communities should know where Christians live

         b. Neighborhoods should be evangelized

         c. Families should be brought to Christ

         d. Reaching the world one community at a time

III. Conclusion

   A. *When Jesus Returned Multitudes Awaited Him (v. 40)*

   B. *One Man Had Been Faithful at Home and Many Believed*

   C. *Let's Make Our Homes Mission Stations*

   D. *Obey Christ's Call for Christian Living at Home*

Jesus of Nazareth Is Passing By

Luke 18:31–43

I. **Introduction**
   A. *Jesus Tells His Disciples They Must Go to Jerusalem (vv. 31–34)*
      1. This journey will lead to the cross
      2. The prophecies concerning Him will be fulfilled
      3. He had been headed toward the cross all His life
   B. *Nearing Jericho They Meet a Blind Beggar*
      1. Not a chance encounter
      2. Reaching one more soul on the way to Calvary

II. **Body**
   A. *The Blind Man's Condition (v. 35)*
      1. The problems he faced
         a. Couldn't see the light
         b. Stumbled often along his way
         c. Had to be led about by others
         d. Lived off the handouts of the world
      2. Pictures the spiritual blindness of all lost people
         a. Jesus said the Pharisees were blind (Matt. 15:14)
         b. Those who followed them were also blind (Matt. 15:14)
         c. Until conversion, all are spiritually blind (1 Cor. 2:14)
         d. Satan blinds people to the Gospel (2 Cor. 4:4)
   B. *The Blind Man's Curiosity (v. 36–37)*
      1. "He asked what it meant"
      2. The noise of this multitude was different
      3. He sensed something special was going on
      4. They told him Jesus of Nazareth was passing by
      5. You may be here today out of curiosity
         a. You've wondered about this church
         b. You sense something different in this place
      6. Jesus of Nazareth is here; He makes the difference
   C. *The Blind Man's Cry (vv. 38–39)*
      1. "Jesus, thou son of David have mercy on me"
      2. He recognized Jesus as the promised son of David

    3. He acknowledged Jesus as the source of mercy
    4. He refused to be intimidated by others
    5. He kept on crying out until the answer came
  D. *The Blind Man's Conversion (vv. 40–43)*
    1. Jesus invited him to come near
      a. He invites all people to come to Him
      b. He instructed others to do their part
      c. We should be bringing people to Jesus
    2. "What wilt thou have me to do?"
    3. The blind man's response to the Lord's question
      a. He called Jesus "Lord"
      b. He believed Jesus could restore his sight
    4. "Receive thy sight: thy faith hath saved thee"
      a. Faith brought the blind man sight
      b. Faith saved him and brought eternal life

III. Conclusion
  A. *Jesus of Nazareth Is Passing By*
  B. *What Do You Want Him to Do?*
  C. *Faith Will Bring His Mercy and Salvation to You*

The Writing Is on the Wall

Independence Day   *Daniel 5*

I. **Introduction**
   A. *Great Texts to Celebrate Liberty*
      1. "Proclaim liberty throughout the land" (Lev. 25:10)
      2. "Proclaim liberty to the captives" (Isa. 61:1)
      3. "The truth shall make you free" (John 8:32)
   B. *But We Will Consider a Stern Text for a Challenging Time (Dan. 5)*
      1. Israel is in captivity in Babylon
      2. Belshazzar, the king of Babylon, is celebrating
      3. Mighty Babylon is about to be judged
   C. *Babylon's Judgment*

II. **Body**
   A. *The Drunken Feast (v. 1)*
      1. Belshazzer and his friends have a drinking party
      2. They celebrate but that night Babylon will fall
      3. Who would have thought it?
         a. Mighty Babylon and its splendor
         b. A city of beautiful homes and great defenses
      4. Belshazzar and friends feel safe in their sinful partying
         a. But one is never safe in sin
         b. Sin is the greatest threat to liberty
         c. We cannot continue on our present course and survive
   B. *The Dedicated Vessels (vv. 2–4)*
      1. Drinking led to foolish actions
         a. Alcohol use is our greatest drug problem
         b. Alcohol kills 25 times as many as all illegal drugs
         c. Alcohol use is America's greatest cause of crime
      2. Belshazzar calls for the sacred vessels
         a. Stolen from the temple in Jerusalem
         b. Vessels set apart for the glory of God
         c. They had been prayed over and dedicated to the Lord

    3. Many of our nation's founders were people of faith
       a. They set a new course for nations: a course of liberty
       b. They hoped this nation would bring glory to God
    4. Now many things are out of control
       a. Abortion, alcoholism, AIDS, to name a few
       b. Crime marches on taking more and more victims
       c. Violence reigns in entertainment and life
       d. Millions have no time for God
    5. We need a revival to turn America from ruin and judgment

C. *The Divine Warning (v. 5–29)*
    1. The night of feasting became a night of fear
    2. The night of triumph became a night of terror
    3. There is a point at which sin is judged
    4. The writing on the wall: "*Mene, Mene, Tekel, Upharsin*"
       a. Daniel was called to interpret the writing
       b. Belshazzar had been weighed and found wanting
       c. That night the kingdom would fall

III. Conclusion
A. *The Writing Is on the Wall for America*
    1. We must face up to our sins
    2. We must turn back to God while we have time
B. *Are You Willing to Let America's Needed Revival Begin in You?*

"Nothing"

Philippians 2:3, 4:6;
Luke 1:37; Revelation 3:17

I. **Introduction**
   A. *Every Sermon Has a Subject*
      1. A preacher has to say something
      2. But today I will preach on "nothing"
   B. *Four Important "Nothings" in the Bible*

II. **Body**
   A. *The Nothing of Activity in Christian Service (Phil. 2:3)*
      1. "Let nothing be done through strife or vain glory"
      2. The problem of strife among Christians
      3. Strife hinders the work of Christ
         a. Strife in Corinth (1 Cor. 3:1–4)
         b. Strife keeps bad company (Gal. 5:20)
         c. Strife is earthly, sensual, devilish (James 3:14–18)
      4. How to overcome strife (Phil. 2:5–8)
         a. Humility overcomes strife
         b. Jesus our example of humility
   B. *The Nothing of Anxiety in Daily Life (Phil. 4:6)*
      1. "Be anxious for nothing"
      2. Often we only obey "Be anxious"
      3. What anxiety does to us
         a. Destroys health
         b. Destroys homes
         c. Destroys dreams and accomplishments
      4. Anxiety does nothing to help us cope tomorrow
      5. Anxiety only drains strength from today
      6. Faith in Christ overcomes anxiety
   C. *The Nothing of Almighty Power (Luke 1:37)*
      1. "For with God nothing shall be impossible"
      2. Consider the challenge to Mary's faith
         a. She was to give birth to Jesus
         b. This to be accomplished without a man
      3. Every obstacle we face is tempered by this "nothing"
      4. Faith grows by acceptance of this "nothing"

111

5. Jeremiah accepted this "nothing" (Jer. 32:27)
6. Accepting Gabriel's "nothing" will chase our doubts away

D. *The Nothing of Apathetic Christianity (Rev. 3:17)*
   1. Laodicea: the lukewarm church of the last days
      a. Focusing on material possessions
      b. Plenty of money, buildings, investments
      c. "I am rich . . . and have need of nothing"
   2. The lukewarm church accomplishes nothing
   3. Souls around this church remain lost
      a. Are we going through religious motions?
      b. "Is it nothing to you, all ye that pass by?" (Lam. 1:12)
   4. How will we answer to God for our apathy?
   5. Vance Havner: "We have no business living ordinary lives in such extraordinary times."

III. **Conclusion**
   A. *Responding to the "Nothings" of the Bible*
      1. Let's put away strife and stop worrying
      2. Let's trust God and overcome apathy
   B. *Let Nothing Hold Us Back from Full Commitment to Jesus*

Pharaoh: Man in Rebellion

From Slavery to Sinai Series   *Exodus 5:1–15*

I. **Introduction**
  A. *Exodus: What a Book!*
    1. A book about God's mercy: making slaves free
    2. A book about God's man: Moses the deliverer
    3. A book about God's might: miracles of deliverance
  B. *Moses and Aaron before Pharaoh*
    1. The people have accepted Moses
    2. He and Aaron go from Goshen to Memphis to meet Pharaoh
    3. Consider the faith this meeting required
  C. *Let My People Go (v. 1)*

II. **Body**
  A. *Pharaoh Rebels against the Plan of God (v. 2)*
    1. "Who is the LORD that I should obey his voice?"
    2. God had spoken and revealed His plan
      a. His plan then was to free Israel from slavery
      b. His plan now is to free us from sin
    3. Pharaoh's rebellion was like man's through the centuries
      a. Adam and Eve in the Garden of Eden
      b. Israel's rebellion in the wilderness
      c. The rejection of Christ by sinners
    4. God has a plan for each of us
      a. His plan includes our salvation (Acts 16:31)
      b. His plan includes obedience to His Word (1 Sam. 15:22)
      c. His plan includes His will for our lives (Col. 1:9)
    5. Don't rebel against God's plan
  B. *Pharaoh Rebels against the Person of God (v. 2)*
    1. "I know not the LORD"
    2. Pharaoh states the condition of his soul
    3. How sad to not know God
      a. To know agriculture but not the One who formed the earth
      b. To know astronomy but not the One who made the stars

        c. To know music but not the One who gives a song
        d. To know art but not the One who created beauty
        e. To know politics but not the King of Kings
    4. We can know the Lord by faith in Christ
    5. Do you know Him?
  C. *Pharaoh Rebels against the People of God (v. 2–15)*
    1. "Neither will I let Israel go"
    2. Pharaoh angry when Israel's burdens are lightened (vv. 4–5)
    3. Israel's burdens increase again
        a. Straw to be withheld (vv. 7–13)
        b. More work to be demanded (vv. 9–14)
    4. Those who love God must also love His people

III. Conclusion
  A. *Rebellion Always Brings Regret*
  B. *Submission to God and His Will Bring Satisfaction and Joy*
  C. *Let God Have His Way in Your Life*

Waiting on God

From Slavery to Sinai Series   *Exodus 5:4–6:23*

I. **Introduction**
  A. *Moses and Aaron before Pharaoh*
     1. The long wait is over; the day arrives
     2. This is the moment for which Moses was born
     3. He had come to the kingdom for such a time (Esther 4:14)
  B. *Pharaoh's Negative Reaction*
     1. Rebelled against the plan of God
     2. Rebelled against the person of God
     3. Rebelled against people of God
  C. *Moses and His People Learn to Wait on God*

II. **Body**
  A. *Daily Duties Continue While Waiting on God (vv. 4–5)*
     1. The people expected immediate release
        a. They stopped working as hard as before
        b. Why should they work hard with deliverance near?
     2. How difficult it is to keep on track while waiting!
     3. The mistake of some who have set dates for Christ's return
        a. Some have quit jobs and waited
        b. Some have spent lavishly and waited
     4. God calls us to be faithful to daily tasks while waiting
  B. *Difficulties May Increase While Waiting on God*

     (vv. 6–19)
     1. No more straw for bricks (vv. 7–8)
     2. More work given to the Israelites (v. 9)
     3. Gathering stubble (v. 12)
     4. Brick production was to stay on target (v. 13)
     5. Punishment for not producing (v. 14)
     6. Our troubles may also increase during waiting times
     7. While waiting, remember that God is faithful
  C. *Some May Become Impatient While Waiting on God (vv. 20–23)*

115

    1. Our waiting may involve others
    2. The complaint of the officers (v. 20)
    3. We must not injure the faith of others
    4. We are to be faith builders while waiting
    5. See the effect of the complainers on Moses (vv. 22–23)
    6. We must encourage others to be patient and trust God

D. *Delays Do Not Mean God Will Fail to Come Through (6:1–2)*
    1. The people doubted and Moses complained
    2. God's promises were unchanged
    3. Deliverance was ahead
    4. The promise at the burning bush would be fulfilled
    5. Never question in the dark what God gave in the light

III. Conclusion

A. *God's Promises to Those Who Wait*
    1. Strength (Ps. 27:14; Isa. 40:31)
    2. Exaltation (Ps. 37:7, 34)
    3. Answers to prayer (Ps. 62:5)
    4. Blessings (Isa. 30:18)

B. *Let Us Be Faithful While Waiting*

C. *Let Us Expect God to Come Through in His Time*

Good News for Burdened People

From Slavery to Sinai Series   *Exodus 6:1–8*

I. Introduction
    A. God Sends Moses to Pharaoh
        1. Pharaoh refuses to let the people go
        2. God renews His pledge of deliverance
    B. God Cares When We Are Troubled

II. Body
    A. God Cares about Our Burdens (v. 6)
        1. "I will bring you out from under the burdens of the Egyptians"
           a. A promise for hurting times
           b. God knows about our pain
        2. The extra labor caused by this call for freedom
           a. Making bricks without straw
           b. Gathering stubble and keeping up the production
           c. Beatings by the taskmasters
        3. Your burdens are important to God
           a. Name your burdens before His throne
           b. He gives grace to help in the time of need (Heb. 4:16)
    B. God Cares about Our Bondage (v. 6)
        1. "I will rid you of their bondage"
        2. Differences between burdens and bondage
           a. Burdens are concerns, cares, problems
           b. Bondage is control by a person or substance
        3. What controls you?
           a. Alcohol or another drug?
           b. A temper that brings you grief?
           c. Fears that limit your usefulness?
    C. God Cares about Our Freedom (v. 6)
        1. "I will redeem you"
        2. The Passover lamb would set them free
        3. We have been redeemed by the blood of Jesus (1 Peter 1:18–20)

    4. Our Lord has come to set us free
       a. Set free by the Scriptures (John 8:32)
       b. Set free by the Savior (John 8:36)
       c. Set free by the Spirit (2 Cor. 3:17)
  D. *God Cares about Our Fellowship (v. 7)*
    1. "I will take you to me for a people"
       a. God would have fellowship with them
       b. He would be their God
    2. He would give them assurance of His presence
    3. He would guide them night and day (the cloud and the fire)
    4. He would provide all their needs
  E. *God Cares about Our Future (v. 8)*
    1. "I will bring you into the land"
    2. God would keep His promises
       a. The promises made to Abraham, Isaac, and Jacob
       b. Their heritage was guaranteed, like ours (1 Peter 1:4)

III. Conclusion
  A. *Let God Lift Those Burdens*
  B. *Come to Christ in Faith and Be Free*

The Plagues Begin

From Slavery to Sinai Series *Exodus 7*

I. **Introduction**
   A. *Back to Pharaoh*
      1. Moses had felt like giving up
         a. His first meeting with Pharaoh brought oppression
         b. The slaves were punished because of his request
      2. God encouraged him so he and Aaron returned (ch. 6)
   B. *The Prophesied Plagues and Their Purposes (vv. 1–5)*
      1. That God's judgments might fall upon Egypt
      2. That God might deliver His people
      3. That the Egyptians might know the Lord

II. **Body**
   A. *The Egyptians Begin to Reap for Their Oppression (v. 4)*
      1. ". . . that I may lay my hand upon Egypt"
      2. The Egyptians were indebted to the Israelites (Gen. 41)
         a. Joseph's interpretation of Pharaoh's dream
         b. Joseph had forecast years of blessing and years of famine
         c. His wise counsel spared Egypt from great suffering
      3. Joseph's family came to Egypt because of the famine
         a. They had multiplied and brought no harm to Egypt
         b. They prospered in Goshen, adding to Egypt's economy
      4. The Egyptians made the Israelites slaves (Ex. 1:8–14)
         a. Taskmasters afflicted God's people
         b. Their lives became bitter because of their bondage

   5. Now God would invoke the law of sowing and reaping (Gal. 6:7)

    a. Egypt would begin to pay for this oppression

    b. We cannot sin and win

  B. *The Lord Begins to Release His People from the Oppressors (v. 4)*

   1. ". . . and bring forth . . . my people . . . out of Egypt"

   2. God's call to Moses from the burning bush (Ex. 3)

    a. He must go to Pharaoh and seek the release of Israel

    b. God would go with him and enable him for the task

   3. Now Pharaoh refuses to let the people go

   4. God announces the first plague (vv. 14–18)

    a. The river will turn to blood

    b. The fish will die and water be undrinkable

   5. The prophecy is fulfilled (vv. 19–25)

   6. Events leading to the release of Israel have begun

  C. *The Egyptians Begin to Realize They Are Dealing with God (v. 5)*

   1. "And the Egyptians shall know that I am the LORD"

   2. When this will happen

    a. When God's power is demonstrated among them

    b. When Israel goes out of Egypt

   3. There were difficult days ahead for Israel and Egypt

    a. The plagues would keep angering Pharaoh

    b. Ultimately these would bring about Israel's release

   4. Finally Pharaoh would say: "Go, serve the Lord" (12:31)

III. Conclusion

  A. *God Is Always at Work on Behalf of His People (Rom. 8:28)*

  B. *God Makes a Way for His People to Be Free*

  C. *God Deserves Our Confidence and Commitment*

Pharaoh and the Frogs

From Slavery to Sinai Series   *Exodus 8:1–15*

I. **Introduction**
   A. *Moses' Persistent Pleading with Pharaoh*
      1. He had a message from God
      2. He kept faithfully declaring it
      3. "Let my people go, that they may serve me"
   B. *Pharaoh Rejects God's Command Again*
   C. *The Plague of the Frogs (vv. 2–6)*
      1. Pharaoh ignores the warning of Moses
      2. Aaron lifts his rod and the plague begins
         a. Frogs were everywhere in Egypt
         b. Speaks of sin and its results in every area of life
         c. There are lessons in this encounter with frogs

II. **Body**
   A. *The Power of the Magicians (v. 7)*
      1. Egyptians worshipped frogs
         a. There was a frog goddess
         b. Embalmed frogs were placed in their tombs
      2. Pharaoh's magicians were called to get rid of the frogs
         a. They could only bring more frogs
         b. Like experts trying to solve today's problems
      3. People can do many things
         a. Build beautiful buildings
         b. Split the atom and travel in space
         c. Discover miracle drugs to cure our ills
      4. Still, our most perplexing problems remain
      5. Ever learning but missing the truth (2 Tim. 3:7–8)
   B. *The Procrastination of Pharaoh (v. 10)*
      1. Moses is called and asked to pray
         a. Even ungodly people know who walks and talks with God
         b. Pharaoh acknowledges that only the Lord can help
      2. Moses asks when he should pray

      3. The strangest reply in the Bible: "Tomorrow"
        a. Pharaoh wants one more night with the frogs
        b. He is like all who put off coming to Christ
        c. Today is the day of salvation (2 Cor. 6:2)
      4. Get right with God today
    C. *The Prayer of Moses (vv. 12–13)*
      1. Moses cried to the Lord
      2. He was specific in his prayer: "because of the frogs"
      3. Puny man calls; mighty God acts
      4. Does your problem seem too difficult to solve?
      5. God answers prayer: the plague ended (v. 13)

III. Conclusion
    A. *After the Frogs Departed, Pharaoh Hardened His Heart (v. 15)*
      1. After their problems are over, many forget God
      2. They harden their hearts to His Spirit
    B. *Remember How God Met You in Your Crisis*
    C. *Respond to His Tender Pleading without Delay*

Compromise

From Slavery to Sinai Series   *Exodus 8, 10*

I. **Introduction**
   A. *The Plagues Finally Get to Pharaoh*
      1. Egypt's water turns to blood (7:19–25)
      2. Frogs appear everywhere (8:1–14)
      3. Lice (8:16–19), the Magicians: "This is the finger of God"
      4. Flies (8:22–24), except in Goshen
   B. *Pharaoh Offers Four Compromises*

II. **Body**
   A. *Go, but Don't Go (8:25)*
      1. "Go ye and sacrifice to your God in the land"
         a. Pharaoh will allow the people to worship God
         b. He insists, however, that they do so in Egypt
      2. Satan offers the same compromise today
      3. Believers are called to a different life
         a. Jesus was not of this world (John 15:18–20)
         b. We are not to be of this world (John 17:14–17)
         c. Deliverance from this evil world (Gal. 1:4)
      4. Moses rejected this compromise (8:27)
   B. *Go, but Don't Go Very Far (8:28)*
      1. "I will let you go"
         a. Not quite the real thing
         b. "Ye shall not go very far away"
      2. Pharaoh only lengthens the chain
      3. You've heard it before
         a. "Don't go off the deep end"
         b. "Don't carry religion too far"
      4. God calls for complete commitment (Rom. 12:1–2)
   C. *Go, but Leave Your Families Here (10:8–10)*
      1. More plagues must come before Pharaoh offers again
         a. Murrain on the cattle (9:1–7)
         b. Boils on the Egyptians (9:8–12)
         c. Hail except in Goshen (9:22–26)
      2. The threat of the plague of locusts (10:4–6)

    3. This compromise is unacceptable
      a. Satan wants our families
      b. Our families ought to serve God with us
        (Josh. 24:15)
  D. *Go, but Leave Your Possessions (10:24–27)*
    1. More plagues to move Pharaoh's heart
      a. Locusts (10:12–20)
      b. Darkness except in Goshen (10:21–23)
    2. "Go ye, serve the LORD"
      a. "Let your flocks and your herds be stayed"
      b. "Let your little ones also go with you"
    3. We've all been offered this compromise
    4. Satan doesn't want God to have our possessions
    5. Moses: "Not an hoof shall be left behind"

III. Conclusion
  A. *Compromise Keeps Us in Bondage*
  B. *Consecration Allows No Compromises*
  C. *Allow Christ to Be Lord of All in Your Life*

Day of Deliverance

From Slavery to Sinai Series   *Exodus 12:1–14*

I. Introduction
  A. *The Heart of Exodus*
    1. Moses at the burning bush looked to this day
    2. The meetings with Pharaoh culminate in this day
  B. *The Importance of the Day of Deliverance*
    1. For Jews: the Passover
    2. For Christians: a type of the sacrifice at Calvary
    3. Moody: "One of the most important chapters in the Bible."
  C. *Pleading and Plagues Fail: Deliverance Must Come By Blood*

II. Body
  A. *The First of Months (vv. 1–2)*
    1. Deliverance by blood to mark a new beginning
    2. The years in Egypt would not count anymore
    3. F. B. Meyer: "Our life before conversion is not reckoned with God."
    4. If you are not living for Christ, you are wasting time
    5. The cry of many hearts: "If only I could begin again"
    6. We begin again through new birth (John 3:3–16)
  B. *Faith in the Blood of the Lamb (vv. 3–7)*
    1. Deliverance from death depended on the blood of a lamb
    2. The choice of the lamb
      a. A male of the first year
      b. Perfect and without blemish (1 Peter 1:18–19)
      c. Christ the perfect One (Heb. 7:26)
      d. Christ the Lamb of God (John 1:29)
      e. The Lamb in heaven (Rev. 5:8; 7:9–17; 19:7–10; 21:8, 23)
    3. The whole assembly shall kill it; one lamb in God's sight
    4. Striking the blood on the door posts
      a. Hyssop: the commonest of plants, speaks of simple faith

        b. The two side posts: upper for God; sides for man
        c. Pictures the cross
    5. This would secure safety for the firstborn of Israel
    6. "When I see the blood, I will pass over you" (Ex. 12:13)

C. *Feeding on the Lamb (vv. 8–11)*
    1. The blood of the lamb for safety
    2. The meat of the lamb for strength
    3. How they were to eat the lamb
        a. Roast with fire: the judgment of the cross
        b. With unleavened bread: Christ's purity
        c. With bitter herbs: the sufferings of Christ
        d. With loins girded: ready to go, to serve
        e. With staff in hand: pilgrims here below
        f. With shoes on their feet: ready to walk in His strength

III. Conclusion
    A. *Provisions in Christ's Death for Us All*
        1. For forgiveness of our sins
        2. For justification
        3. For overcoming in daily life
    B. *Jesus Is All You Need*

Feeding on the Lamb

rom Slavery to Sinai Series   *Exodus 12:8–11*

I. **Introduction**
   A. *Slaves Made Free by the Blood of a Lamb*
      1. The firstborn of Egypt died that night
      2. The firstborn of Israel spared by the sprinkled blood
      3. F. B. Meyer: "They not only rested on the blood thus sprinkled, but also on the distinct promise of God. All under the blood were safe."
   B. *These Delivered Ones Were also to Eat the Lamb*

II. **Body**
   A. *They Were to Feed on the Lamb for Strength*
      1. "And they shall eat the flesh in that night"
      2. The meat of the lamb was to give them strength
         a. This would be a stressful night
         b. There were many difficulties ahead
         c. They would need strength for the journey
      3. We feed on the Lamb by taking in God's Word
      4. Christ strengthens us for every task (Phil. 4:13)
   B. *They Were to Feed on the Lamb for Spiritual Depth*
      1. Many lessons connected with this meal
      2. The lamb was to be roasted with fire
         a. Fire speaks of judgment
         b. All Egypt was under judgment that night
         c. Israel's judgment had fallen on the lambs
         d. Christ our Lamb has borne our judgment on the cross
      3. They were to eat unleavened bread
         a. Leaven, in the Bible, speaks of evil
         b. All evil must be put away from them
         c. Speaks of our sinless Savior
      4. The meal contained bitter herbs
         a. Reminded them of the bitterness of bondage
         b. Reminds us of the sufferings of Christ
      5. "Eat not of it raw, nor sodden at all with water"
         a. This lamb must feel the heat: speaks of God's wrath

        b. Christ has taken the heat for us (2 Cor. 5:21)

        c. This message must not be watered down

    6. "Let nothing remain": a finished sacrifice

  C. *They Were to Feed on the Lamb for Service (v. 11)*

    1. How they were to eat this meal

        a. With their loins girded: ready to go where the Lord would lead them

        b. With their shoes on their feet: no delays when the call came to move

        c. With staff in hand: they would be strangers on the way

    2. We must also obey our marching orders (Matt. 28:18–20)

    3. There are lands to conquer and people to reach

III. **Conclusion**

  A. *Are You Feeding on the Lamb?*

    1. If not, you'll be weak

    2. Start feeding on Jesus

  B. *Christ Will Be Adequate for the Most Difficult Journey*

Through the Red Sea

From Slavery to Sinai Series   *Exodus 14*

I. **Introduction**
   A. *Exodus: the Going Out of the Children of Israel*
      1. Delivered by the hand of God (13:14)
      2. Pictures our salvation
         a. Rescued from the bondage of sin
         b. Delivered by the blood of the Lamb of God
   B. *God's Guides*
      1. A pillar of a cloud by day
      2. A pillar of fire by night
      3. They were traveling in the will of God
   C. *Trouble Came (14:5–9)*
      1. Pharaoh decided he should not have let them go
      2. The Egyptians pursued them with 600 chariots

II. **Body**
   A. *Depression (vv. 10–12)*
      1. The children of Israel were afraid
         a. They were in the habit of fearing Pharaoh
         b. First they prayed, then they pouted
      2. The people complained to Moses
         a. Why have you done this? (v. 11)
         b. Better slaves than graves (v. 12)
      3. Why they turned bitter
         a. They focused on their problems
         b. They forgot God's promises
   B. *Direction (vv. 13–14)*
      1. Moses had a three-point message from God for them
         a. "Fear not"
            (1) What good words!
            (2) God uses them often
                (Gen. 15:1; Isa. 41:10)
         b. "Stand still"
            (1) The opposite of what they wanted to do
            (2) A call from fear to faith (Ps. 46:10)

129

        c. "See the salvation of the Lord"
           (1)   See it now with the eye of faith
           (2)   Faith sees the unseen (2 Cor. 4:18)
     2. Now that they believe, they are ready to act

D. *Divided Waters and Dry Ground (vv. 15–22)*
     1. "Go forward" seemed a contradiction
         a. We cannot move forward until we stand still
         b. Trusting God, they could now move ahead
            (Heb. 11:29)
     2. The cloud that led them confused their enemies
         (vv. 19–20)
     3. When Moses lifted his rod the wind obeyed
         a. A strong east wind divided the waters
         b. The people walked through on dry land
     4. The Gospel in the deliverance of Israel from Egypt
         a. The Passover speaks of the death of Christ
         b. The opened Red Sea speaks of His resurrection

III. **Conclusion**
    A. *Do You Feel Trapped in a Dangerous Place?*
    B. *Stand Still and by Faith See the Salvation of God*
    C. *Now Go Forward*

The Song of the Redeemed

From Slavery to Sinai Series   *Exodus 15:1–21*

I. **Introduction**
   A. *Safely Through the Red Sea*
      1. Delivered people experience God's protection
      2. They have walked through the Red Sea on dry ground
   B. *Their Enemies Were Destroyed*
      1. The Egyptians tried to follow God's people
      2. Miracles cannot be sustained by the flesh
      3. Pharaoh's forces were drowned in sea
   C. *The Children of Israel and Their Song (v. 1)*

II. **Body**
   A. *The Lord Is My Strength (vv. 2–10)*
      1. Memories of slavery
         a. These people had labored long and hard
         b. The sting of whips; the death of their sons
         c. Had longed for freedom but too weak to secure it
      2. Then God intervened and by His strength set them free
      3. Many have found God's strength sufficient (Phil. 4:13)
         a. Struggling with anger, longing for it to cease
         b. Struggling with alcohol, longing for release
         c. Struggling with anxieties, longing for peace
         d. Jesus came and their struggling ceased (2 Cor. 5:17)
   B. *The Lord Is My Song (vv. 11–12)*
      1. "Who is like thee?"
         a. Glorious in holiness
         b. Fearful in praises
         c. Doing wonders
      2. When God becomes your song
         a. Not just the supreme ruler, but your Savior, Redeemer

        b. Not just somebody up there, but the One in your heart

        c. Not just the ruler of the planets, but of your plans

    3. Our God gives us a song

        a. The world needs to hear this song

        b. Let them hear God's song in you

C. *The Lord Is Become My Salvation (vv. 13–19)*

    1. "The Lord in mercy hast led forth the people"

    2. Praise God in song

        a. For His mercy

        b. For His leading

        c. For who He is

        d. For His guidance

        e. For His holiness

        f. For His salvation

III. Conclusion

A. *The Lord Shall Reign Forever and Ever (v. 18)*

    1. Our salvation is eternal

    2. We will reign with Christ forever

B. *Do You Have a Song in Your Heart?*

C. *Let the Whole World Hear*

From Bitterness to Blessing

From Slavery to Sinai Series   *Exodus 15:22–27*

I. **Introduction**
   A. *A Company of Singing Former Slaves*
      1. They have been set free from slavery
      2. Their enemies have perished in the Red Sea
      3. We should have a similar song
   B. *Onward to Canaan*
      1. Moses leads his people into the wilderness
      2. Our Lord knows the way through the wilderness
      3. Great lessons in the wilderness journeys

II. **Body**
   A. *The Bitter Waters of Marah (v. 23)*
      1. Three days into the wilderness and out of water
         a. Containers filled before leaving Egypt exhausted
         b. Our hearts need replenishing all along the way
      2. There was water at Marah, but it was bitter
      3. We may have bitter experiences in this wilderness
         a. Israel disappointed; expected all to go well
         b. We all have trials on the journey (John 16:33)
      4. This trial came in the path of God's leading
   B. *The Bitter Words against Moses (v. 24)*
      1. The people murmured against Moses
      2. Bitter experiences should not make us bitter
         a. When we become bitter we cannot be blessed
         b. Bitter people cannot bless others
      3. Saul was bitter toward David
      4. The prodigal's brother was bitter about his return
      5. God's word to bitter people
         a. Husbands should not be bitter (Col . 3:19)
         b. Bitterness is earthly, sensual, devilish
            (James 3:14–16)
         c. Bitterness spoils our witness (Heb. 12:12–15)
   C. *Moses and His Plea (v. 24)*
      1. Moses cried to the Lord
      2. Pray when others criticize you
      3. Moses didn't know what to do, so he prayed
      4. God promises wisdom to those who ask
         (James 1:5)

D. *God and His Tree (v. 25)*
  1. The Lord showed him a tree
  2. Moses cast the tree into the waters
  3. The tree made the waters sweet
     a. The tree had been there all the time
     b. The tree speaks of the tree of Calvary
     c. Remember the cross when facing bitter experiences
  4. The cross sweetens the bitter times in life

III. Conclusion
  A. *Are You Thirsty of Soul?*
  B. *Come to Jesus and Drink the Sweet Water of Eternal Life*
  C. *Let God Change Your Bitterness to Blessing*

The Hold Up

From Slavery to Sinai Series   *Exodus 17:8–16*

I. **Introduction**
  A. *After Water from the Rock Came War*
    1. The children of Israel were refreshed and rejoicing
    2. Trouble followed this great triumph
    3. In this world we have tribulation (John 16:33)
  B. *The Attack of Amalek*
    1. Joshua leads a select force into battle
    2. Moses, Aaron, and Hur oversee the conflict from a hill
  C. *What Does This Battle Have to Do with Our Church?*

II. **Body**
  A. *We Are in a Battle (v. 10)*
    1. The forces of evil are arrayed against us (Eph. 6:10–12)
    2. Mistaken ideas about the work of a church
      a. We are not here just to preach and teach
      b. We are not here just to raise money
      c. We are not here just to run programs
    3. We are here to do battle with the Enemy
      a. Eternal issues are at stake
      b. Souls hang in the balance
      c. Standards of righteousness are being compromised
      d. Foundations of decency are crumbling
    4. We are equipped to win this battle
      a. The power of the Gospel (Rom. 1:16)
      b. The power of the Holy Spirit (1 John 4:4)
      c. The armor provided us (Eph. 6:13–16)
    5. Ultimate victory is sure (1 Cor. 15:57–58)
  B. *We May Become Weary in the Battle (vv. 11–12)*
    1. Israel's secret weapon in the war with Amalek
      a. When Moses held up his hands Israel prevailed
      b. When Moses let down his hands Amalek prevailed
    2. Moses arms became weary, allowing Amalek an advantage

    3. Your pastor sometimes becomes weary

    4. Fatigue is associated with ministry

       a. The fatigue that follows preaching

       b. The fatigue that follows long hours of study

       c. The fatigue that comes from spiritual conflict

    5. Each one of us sometimes fights fatigue

    6. What can we do to win on our weak days?

  C. *We Can Hold Up the Hands of Those Who Are Weary*
     (v. 12)

    1. A stone was provided so that Moses could rest

    2. Aaron and Hur held up Moses' hands

    3. How we can hold up weary hands

       a. By praying for one another

       b. By refusing to criticize one another

       c. By encouraging one another

       d. By faithfully worshipping with one another

       c. By joining together to win people to Christ

III. Conclusion

  A. *Aaron and Hur Held Up Moses' Hands All Day Long*

  B. *Israel Won the Battle (v. 13)*

  C. *Let's Hold Up Weary Hands and Gain the Victory*

Bread from Heaven

From Slavery to Sinai Series   *Exodus 16*

I.   **Introduction**
  A.   *Moses Leads the Promised Seed toward the Promised Land*
    1.   These are the descendants of Abraham
    2.   They are headed to the land promised to him
    3.   God will not let them starve in the desert
  B.   *Manna for Murmuring People*

II. **Body**
  A.   *The Murmuring of the People (vv. 2–3)*
    1.   The people become hungry and start to complain
    2.   Who are these murmuring people
      a.   Had been slaves but now were free
      b.   Had been trapped but then triumphed
      c.   Had been thirsty, but were given water
    3.   What their grumbling did to them
      a.   Made them say things they did not mean (v. 3)
      b.   Made them exaggerate the facts (v. 3)
      c.   Made them doubt their dearest friend (v. 3)
    4.   God heard their murmuring (v. 4)
    5.   Their murmuring was really against God (v. 8)
  B.   *The Mercy of God (v. 4)*
    1.   "I will rain bread from heaven"
      a.   Not the fire and brimstone they deserved
      b.   How gracious and merciful is our Lord!
    2.   His grace and mercy spare us each day
    3.   We have sinned against God but He is merciful
    4.   Only the Lord's mercy keeps us from destruction (Lam. 3:22–23)
    5.   The Lord's mercies are new every morning (Lam. 3:22–23)
    6.   God was merciful to these murmuring people
    7.   He promised them bread from heaven (v. 4)
  C.   *The Manna from Heaven (vv. 5–36)*
    1.   Manna described (vv. 14–16)
    2.   The manna as a type of Christ (John 6:32–33)

    a. Came down from heaven (v. 4)
    b. Came to the wilderness of sin (v. 1)
    c. Came as a free gift from God (v. 4)
    d. Came as a small thing (v. 14; Phil. 2:5–7)
    e. Was not recognized for what it was
       (John 1:10–12)
    f. Was sufficient for each day's need (v. 18)
    g. Was gathered by stooping (v. 17)
    h. Was white, speaking of purity
       (v. 31; 2 Cor. 5:21)
    i. Was sweet to taste (v. 31)
    j. Is now in heaven (Rev. 2:17)

III. Conclusion

    A. *God Fed That Grumbling Crowd Bread and Meat*
    B. *Christ Comes to Unhappy People to Satisfy Their Spiritual Hunger*
    C. *Receive the Bread from Heaven by Faith and Live*

When Water Flowed from a Rock

From Slavery to Sinai Series   *Exodus 17:1–7*

I. Introduction

A. *Lessons for Slaves Set Free*
   1. God cares when we are in trouble
   2. God sends help in the time of need
   3. God provides when it seems impossible

B. *Lessons Unlearned by the Children of Israel*
   1. At Marah, God had sweetened the bitter water
   2. When out of food, God gave them meat and manna
   3. At Rephidim, they ran out of water and despaired
   4. They forgot God's faithfulness in the past
   5. They blamed Moses for their problem

C. *The Miracle at Rephidem*

II. Body

A. *The Prayer of Moses (v. 4)*
   1. Angry people talk of stoning Moses
      a. Easy to blame others for our problems
      b. Anger causes us to attack even those we love
   2. "What shall I do unto this people?"
      a. Moses didn't know what to do
      b. Moses knew where to go with this problem
   3. Others who have fled to God in crises
      a. Hezekiah threatened by Sennacherib (2 Kings 19)
      b. Daniel threatened by Darius (Dan. 6)
      c. Paul and Silas in prison (Acts 16:25–32)
   4. On the darkest day, God makes a way
   5. Let us take our crises to Christ (Heb. 4:15–16)

B. *The Provision of God (vv. 5–6)*
   1. Moses must lead his people to the rock in Horeb
      a. Moses must take his rod in his hand
      b. Moses must strike the rock expecting water
   2. The rock is a symbol of the Lord
      a. Moses' rock (Deut. 32:4)
      b. David's rock (Ps. 18:1–2)
      c. Isaiah's rock (Isa. 32:1–2)
   3. A rock is strong and durable

139

      a.   The wise man built on the rock (Matt. 7:25)

      b.   The church is built on the rock (Matt. 16:18)

    4.   The smitten rock pictures Christ on the cross

      a.   Christ smitten for us (Isa. 53:3–5)

      b.   Water flowed from the smitten rock (Ps. 105:41)

      c.   Living water flows from the cross

C. *The Peculiar Names (v. 7)*

    1.   Massah: the place of trials

    2.   Meribah: the place of quarreling

    3.   Are you living at Massah or at Meribah?

    4.   See Christ smitten for you and find peace

III. Conclusion

A. *Living Water for Thirsty Souls*

B. *The Last Invitation in the Bible a Call to Drink (Rev. 22:17)*

C. *Accept Our Lord's Invitation Today*

Jethro Meets Jehovah

From Slavery to Sinai Series   *Exodus 18:1–12*

I. Introduction
    A. *Life's Greatest Adventure*
        1. Knowing God in a personal way
        2. Finding and doing God's will
    B. *What Was Missing from Moses' Life: His Wife and Children*
    C. *Moses Sees His Family Coming to Be with Him*
        1. His joy at seeing his wife and children
        2. His responsibility to Jethro, his father-in-law

II. Body
    A. *Moses' Public Image (vv. 1–7)*
        1. Moses had fled from Egypt to Midian
            a. His marriage to Zipporah
            b. They had two sons: Gershom and Eliezer
        2. The call of Moses and his return to Egypt
            a. Zipporah complained so he sent her home
            b. Word reached Zipporah of Moses' success
        3. The public has an image of each of us
            a. The world is watching
            b. Our families are watching too
        4. What God did for Moses because he was faithful
            a. Made him a leader of his people
            b. Reunited his family
    B. *Moses' Personal Witness (v. 8)*
        1. Moses told Jethro what God had done for him
            a. How God had delivered them from Egypt
            b. How God had supplied water, meat, and manna
        3. We should tell others of God's blessings to us
            a. We should never tire of telling of God's faithfulness
            b. We ought to share God's blessings at every opportunity
        4. An ounce of testimony is worth a pound of argument

      5. When did you last tell anyone of God's goodness to you?
- C. *Moses Persuades Jethro to Trust Jehovah (vv. 9–12)*
    1. Jethro was moved by what God had done for Moses
    2. Jethro speaks: "Blessed be the LORD"
    3. Jethro is convinced: "Now I know"
    4. Jethro is converted: his sacrifice, the evidence of faith
    5. Jethro had been a priest of a false God
    6. Never conclude that anyone is unreachable

III. Conclusion
- A. *Will Your Family Circle Be Unbroken?*
- B. *What Members of Your Family Still Need Jesus?*
- C. *Never Give Up on Any of Them*
- D. *Remember Jethro . . . and Expect Them to Come to Christ*

Jethro's Plan

I. **Introduction**
   A. *Meet Jethro: New Convert*
      1. It was a good day when Moses came his way
      2. Moses' testimony brought his father-in-law to the Lord
   B. *How Long Must a New Believer Wait to Serve*
      1. Some new converts begin to serve immediately
      2. Jethro made an early important contribution
      3. Jethro had a plan

II. **Body**
   A. *The Need for Jethro's Plan (vv. 13–18)*
      1. Jethro observed Moses ministering
         a. People stood in line to get advice
         b. They came from morning until night
      2. Jethro saw that Moses needed a better plan
         a. The number coming was so great
         b. Each person coming needed attention
         c. Moses and the people were exhausted
      3. Jethro advised Moses to get organized
      4. Good organization is also needed in a church
         a. Organizing the early church (Acts 6:1–4)
         b. Appointing the first deacons (Acts 6:5–6)
      5. Overloaded leaders are ineffective
      6. Shared responsibility makes the load lighter
      7. Proper organization increases outreach
   B. *Those Needed to Work Jethro's Plan (v. 21–23)*
      1. Able men: able to understand and impart God's Word
      2. Men who fear God: men of faith (Heb. 11:6)
      3. Men of truth: speaking the truth in love (Eph. 4:15)
      4. Men who hate covetousness (1 Tim. 6:10–11)
      5. Requirements for men to serve in the church (Acts 6:5)
         a. Men of honest report
         b. Men full of the Holy Spirit
         c. Men of wisdom

143

C. *The Blessing of Jethro's Plan in Action (vv. 22–27)*
   1. Moses chose able men and put them to work
      a. Rulers of thousands
      b. Rulers of hundreds
      c. Rulers of fifties
      d. Rulers of tens
   2. These judged the people continually
   3. The most difficult cases were brought to Moses
   4. Moses finally got everyone involved
   5. How involved are you in serving God?

III. Conclusion
   A. *God's Call to Active Duty Comes to All Believers*
   B. *How Active Are You?*
   C. *You Must Be Involved to Be Blessed*

Good Words

From Slavery to Sinai Series   *Exodus 19:8*

I. **Introduction**
   A. *Arriving at Mt. Sinai*
      1. A place of memories for Moses: his call
      2. God's promise that he would serve Him there
         (Ex. 3:12)
   B. *God's Challenge to His People (vv. 3–6)*
      1. Reminding them of His deliverance (vv. 3–4)
      2. Blessings tied to obedience
         a. "If ye will obey my voice"
         b. "Ye shall be a peculiar treasure unto me"
         c. "A kingdom of priests, an holy nation"
   C. *The Good Words of the People (v. 8)*

II. **Body**
   A. *These Words Call for Full Surrender*
      1. "All the people answered together, and said, 'All'"
         a. The people spoke as one
         b. They were all of one accord
         c. They agreed on doing all the Lord asked them to
            do
      2. They put aside their differences
         a. This always brings blessing (Ps. 133:1–2)
         b. Reminds us of the Day of Pentecost (Acts 2)
      3. Willing to put aside personal preferences
         a. Said they would seek only God's will
         b. Jesus the example of this in Gethsemane
            (Matt. 26:36–46)
   B. *These Words Call for Faith*
      1. "All that the LORD hath spoken"
      2. They believed God had spoken
         a. Some doubt that God has spoken to men
         b. Some reject the Bible as God's revelation
         c. These people were confident God had spoken
            to Moses
      3. What God has said to all people today
         a. We are all sinners (Rom. 3:10–23)
         b. Sin brings death (Rom. 6:23)

145

    c. Jesus loves sinners and died for us (Rom. 5:8)
    d. Jesus arose from death and invites sinners to salvation (Rom. 10:9)
    e. Sinners who call on Jesus in faith are saved (Rom. 10:13)
  4. Are you willing to come in faith to Jesus?
C. *These Words Call for Follow Through*
  1. "We will do"
    a. Not enough to say we believe (James 2:14)
    b. Faith without works is dead (James 2:20)
  2. The Prodigal arose and went to his father (Luke 15:18–21)
  3. The Philippian jailer believed and was saved (Acts 16:30–34)
  4. Act in faith on what God has said in His Word

III. **Conclusion**
A. *Good Words Were Spoken but Their Promise Was Broken*
  1. God spoke to them as promised (Ex. 20–31)
  2. The people began worshipping Aaron's golden calf (Ex. 32)
  3. Breaking their covenant brought chastening
B. *Did You Once Make Important Commitments to God?*
  1. Did you speak words of faith and full surrender?
  2. Have you failed to carry through?
C. *Return to the Lord and Receive His Forgiveness*
D. *Follow Through on Those Old Commitments Now*

The God Who Is There

Deuteronomy 4:29

I. Introduction
  A. *What Deuteronomy Is All About*
  1. Getting ready to enter the Promised Land
  2. A new generation of Israelites
  a. Unbelief caused the death of the former generation
  b. They had doubted the promises of God
  B. *Moses Prepares His People for the Future*
  1. Looking backward at blessings and chastening
  2. Restating the fundamentals of the faith
  3. Preparing for tough times ahead
  C. *In the Time of Trouble, God Is Available*

II. Body
  A. *God Is Available*
  1. Seek the Lord and find Him
  2. What good news!
  a. There is hope
  b. Prayers really are answered
  c. God is alive
  3. This is the best news of all
  a. Better than announcing a cure for cancer
  b. Better than an end to violence and crime
  c. Better than acquiring great wealth
  4. This news tells us something about God
  a. Not only the creator; He cares
  b. Not only the Lord; He loves us
  c. Not only supreme; He sympathizes
  B. *God Is Available to Sinners and Backsliders*
  1. This text describes God's character
  a. A prophetic text; these would backslide
  b. Some would become idolaters
  2. How Jesus demonstrated this availability in His ministry
  a. He was available to beggars
  b. He was available to lepers
  c. He was available to the thief on the cross

147

      d.   He was available to the empty rich

      e.   He was available to children

   3. Jesus Christ is available to you

D. *God Is Available to Those Who Seek Him with All Their Hearts*

   1. "With all thy heart and with all thy soul"

   2. "When ye shall search for me with all your heart" (Jer. 29:13)

   3. Promises for those who seek righteousness (Matt. 5:6)

      a. "Blessed are they"

      b. "They shall be filled"

   4. No room here for hypocrisy or playing church

   5. A seeking Savior meeting a seeking sinner brings salvation

III. Conclusion

A. *Will You Come to Jesus with All Your Heart?*

B. *Those Who Come in Faith Are Never Turned Away (Rom. 10:9,13)*

Strength for the Day

Deuteronomy 33:25

I. Introduction
   A. *Delivered People about to Enter the Promised Land*
      1. Delivered by blood (the Passover)
      2. Led safely through the Red Sea
      3. Pictures all believers today
   B. *The Last Words of Moses to His People*
      1. Words of warning and promise
      2. Moses prepares them for their promised home
   C. *Assurance to Asher for All His Days*

II. Body
   A. *God Knows All Our Days (v. 25)*
      1. "As thy days"
      2. Asher may have difficult days ahead
         a. Days of toil and trial
         b. Days of temptation and tears
      3. Here is a promise for every occasion
      4. God knows the future from the foundation of the world
         a. Secrets (Matt. 13:35)
         b. The kingdom prepared (Matt. 25:34)
         c. The Lamb slain (Rev. 13:8)
         d. Persecutions of believers (Luke 11:50)
      5. Nothing is hidden from God
   B. *God Knows the Limit of Our Strength (v. 25)*
      1. He must know this in order to equip us for each day
      2. Our Lord knows the breaking point
      3. He will not allow anything to go beyond it
      4. He knows those days when you feel at the end of yourself
         a. Tired, nervous, bewildered
         b. Tempted, discouraged, near giving up
         c. Satanic opposition and oppression
      5. Best of all, He cares

    C. *God Compensates for Our Weakness with His Strength (v. 25)*
- 1. Promises of strength for the weak:
  - a. "He shall strengthen thine heart" (Ps. 27:14)
  - b. "Shall renew their strength" (Isa. 40:31)
  - c. "I will strengthen thee" (Isa. 41:10)
- 2. Take His strength each day by faith
- 3. His strength is sufficient for all we face (Phil. 4:13)

III. Conclusion
    A. *Consider the Cross*
- 1. The pain, the mocking, the scorn
- 2. Our trials are small in comparison
- 3. All this agony because He loves us

    B. *Remember the Resurrection*
- 1. Here is the source of our strength
- 2. Resurrection power: sufficient for all of our needs

Faith Brought the Walls Down

Joshua 6:1–20; Hebrews 11:30

I. Introduction

A. *Joshua's Great Challenge*
1. He replaces Moses
2. The flooded Jordan must be crossed
3. Israel must be led into Canaan

B. *Miracles Begin at Once (3:9–17)*
1. The Jordan River opens before them and closes behind them
   a. Reminds them of the Red Sea
   b. Confirms Joshua's authority under God
2. Another miracle needed to conquer Jericho

C. *Joshua Tested as a Man of Faith*

II. Body

A. *The Opportunity of Faith (vv. 1–2)*
1. Jericho stands in the way of the conquest of Canaan
   a. It is a strong, walled city
   b. The defenders are mighty men of valor
2. Humanly speaking the options were clear
   a. Scale the walls
   b. Beat down the gates
   c. Tunnel underneath at night
3. Faith offered an alternative, just as in salvation
4. Joshua's faith builder (5:13–15)
   a. Encounter with an angel
   b. The captain of the Lord's host
5. The promise: "I have given into thine hand Jericho"
6. God's promise made the victory sure

B. *The Obedience of Faith (vv. 3–14)*
1. A strange battle plan was given to Joshua
   a. Compass the city once a day for six days
   b. The seventh day, compass the city seven times
   c. When the priests blow their ram's horns all are to shout
2. Think of the faith required by this plan

151

     3.   All of God's blessings come by faith
         a.   Our salvation comes by faith (Eph. 2:8–9)
         b.   Faith brings answers to prayer (James 1:6–8)
     4.   Faith requires obedience
         a.   The healing of Naaman the leper (2 Kings 5)
         b.   Servants carrying pots for wine at Cana (John 2:1–11)
     5.   Paul's prayer: "Lord, what wilt thou have me to do? (Acts 9:6)
     6.   How strange this must have appeared to those in Jericho!
     7.   The world doesn't understand obeying in faith
  C.   *The Overcoming Power of Faith (vv. 15–20)*
     1.   The seventh day was the day of victory
         a.   They marched around the city seven times
         b.   The priests blew their trumpets
         c.   The people shouted and the walls fell flat
     2.   Victory comes in God's time and in His way

III.   Conclusion
  A.   *What Is Your Greatest Obstacle?*
  B.   *Expect to Overcome Through the Power of Christ*
  C.   *He Has Won the Greatest Victory at the Cross*
  D.   *Trust Him to Bring Victory to You*

A Text for Troubled Hearts

Series on Heaven   *John 14:1–6*

I. Introduction
  A. *A Text That Meets Us in the Tough Times of Life*
    1. Most familiar set of verses in the New Testament
    2. Often associated with death and funerals
    3. Its message reaches to every troubled heart
  B. *A Text That Takes Us from Trouble to Triumph*

II. Body
  A. *A Text That Calls Us to Peace in Times of Peril*
    1. The disciples and Jesus in the Upper Room (John 13)
      a. They have come to Jerusalem for the Passover
      b. A pleasant meal; the precious fellowship
      c. Jesus washes the disciples' feet
    2. Jesus reveals the tough times ahead
      a. Judas will betray Him (13:21–30)
      b. Peter will deny Him (13:36–38)
    3. There are tough times ahead for us all
      a. "In the world you will have tribulation" (John 16:33)
      b. Most go through things they didn't think they would
      c. Many go through things they didn't think they could
    4. Even then: "Let not your heart be troubled"
    5. We can be peaceful in perilous times
  B. *A Text That Calls Us to Trust in Times of Trouble*
    1. *Believe*: a life changing word
      a. To believe is to exercise faith
      b. Believe and be saved (Acts 16:31)
      c. Believe and get your prayers answered (Mark 9:23)
    2. "Ye believe in God"
      a. Faith that God exists; that He is the Creator
      b. Faith that God is in control
    3. "Believe also in me"
      a. Believe that Jesus came to save sinners

b. Believe that Jesus died to pay for our sins
c. Believe that Jesus arose from the dead
d. Act on this belief: trust Christ for salvation
e. Rest your future in His hands

C. *A Text That Calls Us to Look Beyond Life's Difficulties*
   1. "In my Father's house are many mansions"
      a. All trouble here is temporary
      b. Trials are only "for a season" (1 Peter 1:6)
      c. The best is yet to come (Phil. 1:21–23)
      d. Heaven awaits all believers (2 Cor. 5:8)
   2. "I go to prepare a place for you"
      a. What a wonderful place heaven must be!
      b. Look beyond your heartaches to heaven
   3. "I will come again"
      a. The blessed hope of every believer
      b. Are you ready for His return?

III. Conclusion
   A. *Heaven Is a Prepared Place for Prepared People*
   B. *Are You Prepared for Heaven?*

The Difference

Series on Heaven   *1 Thessalonians 4:13–18*

I. Introduction
   A. *Some Go to Heaven When They Die and Some Don't*
   B. *Some Will Be Ready for Christ's Return and Some Won't*
   C. *Here Is a Text to Help Us Know the Difference*

II. Body
   A. *The Difference between Hope and No Hope (v. 13)*
   1. Concern about loved ones who die
      a. This is a common concern since all die (Heb. 9:27)
      b. Paul faces the problem and gives answers
   2. We do not sorrow as those who have no hope
      a. Sorrow is normal when loved ones die
      b. Grief is normal; Jesus wept at a grave (John 11:35)
   3. The Christian's grief is different
      a. We have assurance of better things ahead (Phil. 1:21–23)
      b. We know where departed believers have gone (2 Cor. 5:8)
      c. We know we will see them again (v. 17)
   4. Lost people have no hope
   B. *The Difference between Belief and Unbelief (v. 14)*
   1. "If we believe that Jesus died and rose again"
   2. The key to hope is faith
      a. To believe is to trust
      b. More than intellectual assent
      c. Resting securely in Christ who died and rose again
   3. To believe is to be saved (Acts 16:31)
   4. To believe is to be sure of heaven (1 John 5:12–13)
   5. Concerning those who refuse to believe
      a. They have no hope of heaven
      b. They will be lost forever

    C. *The Difference between the First and Second Resur-rections (v. 16)*
        1. What happens when Jesus comes
           a. The Lord descends from heaven with a shout
           b. The voice of the archangel and the trump of God
           c. Jesus returns with those who have gone to heaven
           d. He resurrects their bodies and reunites them
           e. Living believers are caught up and changed (1 Cor. 15:51)
           f. This cloud of Christians departs for heaven
           g. All unbelievers are left
           h. The unbelieving dead are not resurrected
        2. Unbelievers are resurrected later for judgment (Rev. 20:5–15)

III. Conclusion
    A. *Are You Lost and without Hope of Heaven?*
    B. *Join the Different Crowd*
        1. Come as a sinner to Jesus
        2. Receive Him by faith and be ready for heaven and His return

Will We Know Our Loved Ones in Heaven?

Series on Heaven   *1 Peter 1:3–5*

I. Introduction
A. *What Makes the Hope of Heaven Precious?*
   1. We will immediately be there upon death (2 Cor. 5:8)
   2. No sickness, sorrow, nor death there (Rev. 21:1–6)
   3. Jesus will be there (John 14:1–3)
   4. Our inheritance is there (1 Peter 1:4)

B. *Believing Loved Ones Will also Be There*
   1. Separation will be over
   2. We will see them and know them

C. *How Do We Know?*

II. Body
A. *Heaven Is Not a Place of Darkness but of Light (Rev. 21:23–27)*
   1. Jesus was the Light of the World while on earth (John 8:12)
      a. Many found in Him the light of life
      b. Many are still doing so
   2. Heaven has light without the sun or moon (v. 23)
      a. The glory of God lights up Glory
      b. The Lamb is the light of heaven
   3. There is no night there (v. 25)
   4. Hell is the place of darkness (Matt. 8:12)
   5. We will have more light then than now about everything

B. *Heaven Is Not a Place of Blindness but of Sight (1 Cor. 13:12)*
   1. Many are blind on earth
      a. Some are physically blind
      b. Many are spiritually blind (1 Cor. 2:14)
   2. Jesus came to open the eyes of the blind
      a. He opened the eyes of the physically blind
      b. Receiving Him brings spiritual sight (1 Cor. 2:15–16)

157

      3. We shall not know less in heaven, but more

        a. We will know the saints of all the ages

        b. We will know Jesus

        c. Why would we then not know our loved ones?

      4. We will know them when we meet them over there

C. *Heaven Is a Place Where Jesus Makes Things Right (1 Thess. 4:13–18)*

      1. Here is a text of comfort

        a. Comfort for those who have lost loved ones in death

        b. What comfort if they would never know them again?

      2. This entire text speaks of reunion and fellowship

        a. A family reunion without recognition?

        b. Fellowship only with strangers?

      3. We will know our saved loved ones and enjoy heaven with them

III. Conclusion

A. *We Will Fellowship There with the Family of God*

B. *Are You Part of the Family?*

C. *Receive the Savior and Become a Child of God (John 1:12)*

Marriage in Heaven

Series on Heaven   *Revelation 19:6–9*

I. Introduction
   A. We're Going to a Wedding
      1. A scene from heaven
      2. The marriage of the Lamb
      3. While the Tribulation rages on earth
   B. Participants and Plans for the Marriage of the Lamb

II. Body
   A. The Groom (vv. 6–7)
      1. The Groom is Jesus
         a. John the Baptist called Him the Lamb of God (John 1:29)
         b. He is worshipped as the Lamb in heaven (Rev. 5:12)
         c. He is called the Lamb that was slain (Rev. 5:8–12)
      2. Jesus called Himself the Bridegroom (Matt. 9:15)
      3. The parable of the wise and foolish virgins (Matt. 25:1–13)
         a. A parable about the return of Christ
         b. A warning for us all to be ready (v. 13)
      4. An outpouring of praise as the wedding begins (v. 6)
      5. A time for heaven to be glad and rejoice (v. 7)
   B. The Bride (vv. 7–8)
      1. The bride is the church
      2. Every wedding should remind us of Christ and His church
         a. Paul teaching duties of husbands and wives (Eph. 5:22–33)
         b. All drawn from Christ and His bride, the church (v. 32)
      3. Jesus died to pay for the sins of His bride
      4. The Bridegroom's grace makes the bride's gown possible
      5. The bride's gown is made of fine linen
         a. The fine linen is the righteousness of saints
         b. What we weave in time we wear in eternity

C. *The Reception (v. 9)*
1. "The marriage supper of the Lamb"
2. Here is a great feast in heaven
   a. All present at the supper are especially blessed
   b. Good food will evidently be a part of heaven
3. There is good reason to celebrate
   a. A marriage of love (John 3:16)
   b. A marriage that will last forever
4. Perhaps supper music by the angels

III. Conclusion
A. *Our Lord's Invitation to the Marriage Supper (Luke 14:16–24)*
1. The Holy Spirit is still inviting
2. Many are still making excuses
3. The poor, the maimed, the lame, and the blind are still welcome

B. *Accept the Gracious Invitation Today*

Tears Gone Forever

Series on Heaven   *Revelation 21:1–6*

I. Introduction

   A. *Let's Talk about a Neglected Subject: Eternity*
     1. Most of our thoughts center on temporal things
     2. But our time here is short and eternity is long
   B. *Those Who Are Born Again Can Anticipate a Bright Eternity*
     1. Heaven is ahead for the saved
     2. Heaven will be "far better"
   C. *What Believers Have Awaiting Them After Death*

II. Body

   A. *Eternity with Our Savior (v. 3)*
     1. "He will dwell with them"
     2. Faith in Christ begins a wonderful walk with God
     3. Their walk with the Lord continues in heaven
       a. He will dwell with them
       b. They shall be His people
       c. God Himself shall be with them
       d. He will be their God
   B. *Eternity without Tears (v. 3)*
     1. There are many tears here
       a. The first sign of life in a baby—a cry
       b. The disappointments and hurts of childhood
       c. The shattered dreams of the working years
       d. The loneliness and pain of old age
     2. Jesus was a Man of Sorrows (Isa. 53)
       a. Sorrow in Gethsemane (Matt. 26:38)
       b. Weeping at the grave of Lazarus (John 11:35)
       c. Weeping over Jerusalem (Luke 19:41)
     3. God will wipe away all tears
     4. There will be no more sorrow nor crying
   C. *Eternity without Separation (v. 4)*
     1. "There will be no more death"
     2. Death brings separation
       a. Separation of body and spirit (James 2:26)
       b. Separation from friends and loved ones
     3. The last enemy will finally be destroyed (1 Cor. 15:26)

    D. *Eternity without Sickness (v. 4)*
       1. "Neither shall there be any more pain"
       2. Physical infirmities are always with us
       3. In heaven we will enjoy perfect health
         a. No colds nor cancer
         b. No arthritis nor appendicitis
         c. No headaches nor heart attacks
       4. All will be new—including us

III. Conclusion
    A. *A Timely Word from Jesus (v. 6)*
       1. He is the beginning and the end
       2. He offers living water to all who thirst
    B. *Come to Him in Faith and Be Satisfied Forever*

Not

I. Introduction

A. *The Widow Who Thought She Was Going to Die*
1. There was a famine in the land
2. She and her sons were almost out of food
3. Elijah had announced the famine to the king (v. 1)

B. *God Changed This Widow's Negatives into Positives*
1. He moved her from poverty to plenty
2. He brought her from anxiety to assurance
3. Elijah would come from Cherith with help from God

C. *The Widow's Journey from "Have Not" to "Wasted Not"*

II. Body

A. *"I Have Not" (vv. 8–12)*
1. This widow was a woman of faith
2. God was able to communicate with her
   a. She had been expecting Elijah
   b. What would be expected of her?
3. Elijah arrived thirsty and hungry
   a. "Fetch me . . . a little water"
   b. What a relief, he might have asked for food!
4. "Bring me a morsel of bread"
   a. "I have not a cake"
   b. Depression moves in
   c. She sees only death ahead
5. Focus on what you don't have and depression will follow
   a. She had a handful of meal and a little oil
   b. What do you have that God can use?

B. *"Fear Not" (v. 13)*
1. Fear is common to all
2. Fear was the first evidence of the fall (Gen. 3:10)
3. So many kinds of fears may beset us
   a. Fears about our families
   b. Fears about health
   c. Fears about money

    4. Elijah's advice to the worried widow
        a. She was to make that cake: do the routine
            things
        b. But first, she was to make a cake for him
    5. God first (Matt. 6:33)
    6. In giving God priority, we overcome our fears

C. *"The Barrel of Meal Wasted Not" (vv. 14–16)*
    1. Things turned out better than the widow expected
    2. We have all feared things that didn't happen
    3. The widow put God's will first and He provided
        for her
    4. Lessons learned by the widow
        a. God is faithful at all times
        b. We can't out give God

III. Conclusion
    A. *Are Fears Robbing You of the Joy of Living?*
    B. *Trade Your Fears for Faith*
    C. *Give Christ First Place in Your Life*
    D. *He Has Promised to Provide for You*

Isaiah's Metaphors of Christ

Isaiah 32:2

I. Introduction
    A. Isaiah Looks Ahead to the Coming Savior
1. He had prophesied His virgin birth (7:14)
2. He had revealed His many names (9:6)
3. He had written of His coming kingdom (9:7)
4. Now he describes the Man

    B. What Is Jesus Like?

II. Body
    A. He Is Like a Hiding Place from the Wind
1. Speaks of salvation
2. We are all subject to the winds of life
   a. Winds of circumstance that move us
   b. Winds of temptation that allure us
   c. Winds of trouble that try us
3. We need a quiet harbor during high winds
4. Faith in Jesus calms the winds of guilt
5. He receives and forgives all who come to Him (John 6:37)

    B. He Is Like a Covert in the Tempest
1. Speaks of security
2. A covert is a place of refuge
   a. A shelter from storms
   b. A home for the homeless
   c. A stronghold in the time of battle
   d. A sanctuary for those needing peace
3. There are many storms: social, economic, emotional
4. Find shelter from your storm in Jesus

    C. He Is Like Rivers of Water in a Dry Place
1. Speaks of refreshment and satisfaction
2. The world's unfailing search for satisfaction
3. Jesus offered living water
   a. His offer to the woman at the well (John 4:14)
   b. His promise of the Holy Spirit (John 7:37–39)
4. He still offers living water to all today (Rev. 22:17)

    D. *He Is Like the Shadow of a Great Rock in a Weary Land*
- 1. Speaks of rest and refreshment
- 2. Jesus offers rest to all the weary (Matt. 11:28–30)
  - a. Some are weary in fighting temptation
  - b. Some are weary in battling poor health
  - c. Some are weary of financial woes
  - d. Some are weary of family conflicts
- 3. Come to Jesus and find rest
- 4. He will refresh you and give new strength (Isa. 40:31)

III. Conclusion
    A. *Jesus Is an All-Sufficient Savior*
    B. *Jesus Is All We Need*
    C. *Trust Him to Save You Today (Acts 16:31)*

From Cheating to Charity

Luke 19:1–10

I. Introduction
A. *A Crooked Tax Collector Meets Jesus*
1. Jesus was passing through Jericho (v. 1)
2. Zacchaeus met Jesus and was changed
3. The conversion of a man nobody thought would be saved

B. *How It All Began*
1. Zacchaeus, a rich man with a bad reputation
2. Jesus, the sinless Savior, comes to town
3. The struggle of Zacchaeus in coming to Jesus

II. Body
A. *His Downfall (v. 2)*
1. Wealth had Zacchaeus
   a. He was chief among the publicans (tax collectors)
   b. The love of money had made him dishonest
   c. He was considered a traitor by the Jews
2. He must have found his wealth insufficient
   a. His passion for money had left him feeling empty
   b. If you love money, you're sure to be disappointed
3. Zacchaeus probably hoped Jesus could set him free

B. *His Climbing Up (vv. 3–4)*
1. Zacchaeus was of "little stature"
   a. Couldn't see Jesus because of the crowd
   b. H. A. Ironside: "He was a come-shorter."
2. We all come short of the glory of God (Rom. 3:23)
3. Zacchaeus climbed a sycamore tree in order to see Jesus
   a. He wanted to get above the others
   b. Many think they must climb up to get to Jesus
   c. They hope good deeds will gain them favor
   d. They trust religious ceremonies to lift them up
4. Good works avail nothing in achieving salvation
5. We are saved by grace alone (Eph. 2:8–9)

167

    C. *His Coming Down (vv. 5–6)*
1. "Zacchaeus, make haste, and come down"
2. The scene below this climber
   a. Common people: reaching, crowding, listening
   b. The poor, the sick, the sinful, the troubled
   c. He may have thought himself better than these
3. Still, Zacchaeus must come down to be saved
4. He made haste and came down; will you?

    D. *His Opening Up (vv. 6–8)*
1. Zacchaeus opened up his heart (v. 6)
2. He opened up his home (v. 7)
3. He opened up his wallet (v. 8)
4. He opened up his eyes to the needs of others (v. 8)
5. He opened up his mouth to tell of full commitment (v. 8)

III.   Conclusion

    A. *Salvation Came to the House of Zacchaeus (v. 9)*
    B. *Jesus Reveals This Is What He Has Come to Do (v. 10)*
    C. *Let Jesus Bring Salvation to You*

Three People Present Today

1 Corinthians 2:14–3:4

I. Introduction
   A. *Here Is a Sermon for Everyone*
- 1. Some sermons to convert the lost
- 2. Some sermons to feed or correct believers
- 3. This one's for you

   B. *Three Kinds of People*
- 1. The natural man (v. 14)
- 2. The spiritual man (v. 15)
- 3. The carnal man (3:1)

   C. *Who Are These Representative People?*

II. Body
   A. *The Natural Man (v. 14)*
- 1. Paul's message and method (vv. 1–13)
  - a. His message was Christ and Him crucified (v. 2)
  - b. His method was preaching in the power of God (vv. 3–4)
  - c. He wanted to reach the "natural man"
- 2. The natural man has not been born again
  - a. He cannot understand spiritual things
  - b. They are foolishness to him
- 3. The Bible is a dark book to the natural man
- 4. The destiny of the natural man is destruction
- 5. The need of the natural man is salvation
  - a. All people are naturally lost (Rom. 3:23)
  - b. All lost people can be saved (John 6:37; Rom. 10:9, 13)

   B. *The Spiritual Man (v. 15)*
- 1. The spiritual man was once a natural man
- 2. Salvation through faith in Christ transformed him
  - a. Once doomed; now delivered
  - b. Once lost; now found
  - c. Once bound for hell; now bound for heaven
- 3. The Holy Spirit teaches the spiritual man (vv. 11–13)
- 4. The spiritual man discerns (understands) all things
  - a. Sees God at work in the world
  - b. Sees God at work in his or her life

      5. He is not understood by others
         a. The warning of Jesus (John 15:18–20)
         b. Peter's explanation (1 Peter 4:12–14)
      6. The spiritual man has the mind of Christ (v. 16)
  C. *The Carnal Man (3:1–4)*
      1. The carnal man is confused
         a. The natural man lives for the moment
         b. The spiritual man lays up treasures in heaven
         c. The carnal man tries looking both ways
      2. Contradictions of the carnal man
         a. He knows what is right but doesn't do it
         b. He knows the world is lost but clings to it
         c. He is like Lot lingering in Sodom
      3. The carnal man needs full commitment to Christ

III. Conclusion
  A. *Which Person Are You?*
  B. *Christ Will Meet You Where You Are*
  C. *He Will Make You the Spiritual Person You Ought to Be*
  D. *It's Your Move*

What We Need to Know to Grow

Series on Maturity   *2 Peter 3:18*

I.   Introduction
   A.   *God's Great Plan: Birth, Growth, Maturity*
   1.   Many believers never mature as intended
   2.   Too many spiritual babies (1 Cor. 3:1–5)
   B.   *Indications of Spiritual Infancy*
   1.   Griping instead of gratefulness
   2.   Argument instead of action
   3.   Following men instead of the Master
   C.   *How Can One Get on the Grow?*

II. Body
   A.   *We Must Know How to Feed Ourselves (1 Peter 2:2)*
   1.   Proper food for proper growth
   2.   So much available that is not wholesome
      a.   Violence in the news
      b.   Too much entertainment
      c.   Immoral plots in drama
   3.   Each believer must develop a strong devotional life
      a.   Starting the day with God and His Word
           (2 Tim. 2:15)
      b.   Taking time for thanksgiving and prayer
           (Phil. 4:6–8)
      c.   Finding faith-builders for the day
           (Ps. 119:9–11)
   B.   *We Must Know How to Allow Others to Feed Us*
        (Heb. 10:25)
   1.   The importance of the church in maturing
        (Eph. 4:11–16)
      a.   Church attendance is vital to growth
      b.   Gifted people called to feed us
      c.   Christian fellowship to encourage us
      d.   Opportunities for service to strengthen us
   2.   Reading faith-building books
   3.   Expecting God to speak to us through others
   4.   Seeing Christ in the lives of other believers

   C. *We Must Know How to Walk (Gal. 5:16)*
      1. Walk in the Spirit
         a. Grieve not the Spirit (Eph. 4:30)
         b. Quench not the Spirit (1 Thess. 5:19)
      2. Walk in newness of life (Rom. 6:4)
      3. Walk by faith (2 Cor. 6:7)
      4. Walk worthy of the Lord (Col. 1:10)
      5. Walk circumspectly (Eph. 5:15)
      6. Walk in love (Eph. 5:2)
      7. Walk in light (Eph. 5:8)
   D. *We Must Know How to Reproduce (John 15:8)*
      1. Fruit bearing is reproduction
         a. The fruit of a tree is another tree
         b. The fruit of a Christian is another Christian
      2. Andrew led his brother Peter to Jesus (John 1:41)
      3. Three thousand converts at Pentecost (Acts 2:41)
      4. Early believers kept multiplying (Acts 6:7)
      5. Believers who reproduce thrive and grow

III. Conclusion
   A. *Checking Our Devotions, Our Worship, Our Walk, Our Witnessing*
   B. *How Do We Measure Up?*
   C. *Let's Get Back to These Basics of Growth*
   D. *Let's Become Mature Christians*

Identifying Mature Christians

I. Introduction

A. *Peter and the Sufferings and Death of Christ*
1. The precious blood of Jesus (1:18–19)
2. Christ bearing our sins (2:21–25)
3. The just for the unjust (3:18)

B. *Peter's Personal Experience and the Cross*
1. His denials of Christ
2. He didn't want to be identified with Jesus

C. *Peter Explains the Mature Believer's Identity*

II. Body

A. *How Mature Christians Identify with Christ's Sufferings (vv. 1–2)*
1. Growth brings greater appreciation of the sufferings of Christ
   a. "As Christ has suffered for us in the flesh"
   b. He took our suffering upon Himself (Isa. 53:5)
2. Paul takes up the same theme
   a. "I am crucified with Christ" (Gal. 2:21)
   b. Dead with Christ; living with Christ (Rom. 6:8)
3. "Arm yourselves with the same mind"
   a. Christ has won the victory at the cross
   b. Identifying with Him brings daily victory
4. In view of Christ's sufferings, we should forsake sin (v. 2)
5. The will of God should be our goal (v. 2)

B. *How Mature Christians Are Identified by the World (vv. 3–6)*
1. Our past was not good
   a. Lust, drinking, idolatries
   b. Fulfilling the desires of the flesh and mind (Eph. 2:3)
2. Christ changed our lives (2 Cor. 5:17)
3. Some cannot understand this change
   a. They think the change is strange
   b. They speak evil because we choose good

       4. The world sees our light and prefers darkness
       5. We shall be vindicated in judgment (Rom. 14:12)
       6. Believers must always take the long look (v. 7)
- C. *How Mature Christians Identify with Each Other*
    (vv. 8–12)
    1. "Have fervent charity among yourselves"
       a. We should be identified by our love
       b. This love should be fervent (intense)
    2. What this love does
       a. Covers a multitude of sins
       b. Makes hospitality natural
       c. Enables us to give without grudging
    3. We are to minister to each other
       a. God's grace enables us to minister
       b. God is glorified in such demonstrations of love

III. Conclusion

- A. *How Mature Are You?*
    1. What do the sufferings of Christ mean to you?
    2. Does the world see you as a Christian?
    3. Do you love other believers intensely?
- B. *A Fresh Glimpse of the Cross Hastens Maturity*
- C. *Commit Your Life, Your All, to the Crucified One*

Growing through Trials

Series on Maturity   *1 Peter 4:12–14*

I. Introduction
  A. *God's Instruments of Growth*
     1. The Christian life begins with spiritual birth
        (John 3:3–5)
     2. God's plan is birth, growth, and maturity
     3. God uses the Bible, the church, other believers to
        mature us
     4. God also uses trials to bring us to maturity
  B. *Some Truths about Trials*

II. Body
  A. *Why Christians Have Trials (v. 12)*
     1. "Think it not strange"
     2. Christians have trials because we live in a sinful
        world
        a. We are part of a fallen race (Rom. 3:10–23)
        b. We live in a world of turmoil and natural
           disasters
        c. We live in a world of crime, sickness, death
           (Heb. 9:27)
     3. Christians have trials because of the power of
        Satan
        a. We have an adversary: Satan
        b. Consider Satan's attack on Job
        c. The roaring lion (1 Peter 5:8)
     4. Christians are on a collision course with the world
        a. Jesus warned of this conflict (John 15:18–20)
        b. Many have suffered and died for Christ
           (Heb. 11:36–40)
  B. *Why the Christian's Trials Are Different (v. 13)*
     1. We do not suffer alone (Heb. 13:5–6)
     2. We become partakers of Christ's sufferings (v. 13)
     3. We can even find joy in jeopardy (Acts 16:25–32)
     4. There is a design in our difficulties
        (Rom. 8:28–29)
     5. After our trials will come glory (Rom. 8:17–18)

   C. *How Mature Christians React to Their Trials (v. 14)*
      1. "Happy are ye"
         a. Happy even when reproached
         b. God is with us in our trials
      2. Christians may have financial trials
         a. Sometimes we make poor financial decisions
         b. Sometimes financial conditions are out of our hands
         c. Financial trials teach us to care and give (Phil. 4:10)
      3. Christians may have trials concerning health
         a. Song writer Fanny Crosby was blind
         b. Poet Annie Johnson Flint suffered from arthritis
         c. Health problems often teach us to sympathize and pray
      4. Christians may have trials concerning their families
         a. Even the faithful often suffer in this area
         b. These trials teach us to rejoice in the family of God
      5. Christians may have emotional problems
         a. Many find help from Christian counselors
         b. Emotional problems teach us to lean on Jesus

III. Conclusion

   A. *How Are You Doing in God's School of Trials?*
   B. *Are Your Trials Making You Better or Bitter?*
   C. *Look to Jesus in Trials: He Understands and Cares*

The Mature Christian

Ephesians 5:17–33

I. **Introduction**
   A. Maturity *Is a Good Word*
      1. Youth is good but maturity is better
      2. Maturity in nature
         a. A rose in full bloom
         b. A watermelon when red and juicy
         c. A full grown tree offering shade and beauty
   B. *A Mature Christian Has Grown Up in the Faith*
      1. Born again by faith in Jesus
      2. Taught in the Scriptures and able to teach
      3. Matured through suffering and able to comfort
   C. *Recognizing Mature Christians*

II. **Body**
   A. *The Mature Christian's Wisdom (v. 17)*
      1. "Wherefore be ye not unwise"
      2. The world is interested in accumulating knowledge
         a. Education is everything
         b. Ever learning but missing the truth
            (2 Tim. 3:7)
      3. The mature Christian seeks wisdom
         a. Wise ones know what to do with knowledge
         b. Mature Christians know the source of wisdom
            (James 1:5)
      4. Mature Christians find the will of God and do it
         a. "Understanding what the will of the Lord is"
         b. Have you found the will of God for your life?
         c. Do you seek the will of God each day?
         d. Is doing the will of God your delight?
   B. *The Mature Christian's Worship (vv. 18–20)*
      1. Worship should be both private and public
      2. The mature Christian's worship is spiritual
         a. "Be filled with the Spirit"
         b. Not given to forms and ceremonies
         c. Heartfelt and Spirit-directed
      3. The mature Christian's worship is scriptural
         a. "Speaking to yourselves in psalms"
         b. Emotionally submitted to the Scriptures

    4. The mature Christian's worship involves singing
       a. Hymns, spiritual songs, singing
       b. Music is a powerful expression of worship
       c. Music is a part of the worship of heaven
          (Rev. 5:9; 15:3)
    5. The mature Christian's worship comes from a
       grateful heart
       a. "Giving thanks always"
       b. Thanking God for all things (Rom. 8:28–29)

C. *The Mature Christian's Walk (vv. 21–33)*
    1. The mature Christian has learned to submit (v. 21)
       a. "Submitting yourselves one to another"
       b. Jesus is the example (Phil. 2:5–7)
       c. Submission is the opposite of self-will
    2. Submission even in the home (v. 23)
    3. The mature Christian walks in love (v. 25)
    4. The mature Christian represents Christ continually
       (vv. 25–33)

III. Conclusion
    A. *How Long Has It Been Since You Checked Your*
       Growth?
    B. *How Mature Are You?*

Why Grow Up?

Series on Maturity   *Ephesians 4:11–16*

I. **Introduction**
   A. *God Has a Team Assigned to Bring Us to Maturity*
       (v. 11)
       1. The apostles and prophets through their writings
       2. Evangelists teach us the value of soulwinning
       3. Pastors and teachers keep believers strong in faith
       4. These "perfect" or "mature" the saints
   B. *God's Purpose Is to Build Up the Body of Christ*
       (v. 12)

II. **Body**
   A. *Who Is to Do the Work of the Ministry? (v. 12)*
       1. The saints are to do the work of the ministry
           a. Saints are those who have been born again
           b. All believers are to do the work of the ministry
       2. Most churches reverse the divine plan
           a. Pastors do the work of the ministry
           b. Saints come to listen and critique sermons
           c. Congregations seek to perfect the pastors to
               minister
       3. Too many Christians are but paying spectators
       4. What is the result of this backward present plan?
           a. The church moves at a snail's pace
           b. Members miss the blessing of ministry
           c. When the body is not busy it creates busybod-
               ies
       5. We must get back to God's plan: all believers
           ministering
   B. *What Is the Work of the Ministry? (v. 12)*
       1. The ministry is anything that builds up the body of
           Christ
           a. To edify is to build up
           b. What are you doing to edify believers?
       2. The ministry is caring for the afflicted
           a. Comforting the sick and sorrowing
               (1 Thess. 5:11–14)
           b. Visiting the fatherless and widows
               (James 1:27)

3. The ministry is caring for physical needs of believers
   a. Paul distributing to the necessity of saints (Rom. 12:13)
   b. Ministering to the poor saints in Jerusalem (15:25–26)
4. The ministry is caring for the spiritual needs of believers
   a. Ministering to those overtaken by a fault (Gal. 6:1)
   b. Ministering is encouraging one another (Heb. 10:25)
5. Ministering is evangelizing (Acts 8:8)

C. *What Happens When We All Do the Work of the Ministry? (vv. 13–16)*
   1. The church is unified (v. 13)
   2. Believers become Christlike (v. 13)
   3. Christians become solid in faith and doctrine (v. 14)
   4. The church is protected from false teaching (v. 14)
   5. Love flows through all preaching and teaching (v. 15)
   6. The church grows and is known for fellowship and love (v. 16)

III. Conclusion

A. *Let Us Return to God's Plan for His Church*
B. *Let Leaders Perfect (Mature) the Saints to Serve*
C. *A Ministering Church Will Reach Its Community for Christ*

The Pastor and the Church

Series on Maturity   *Ephesians 4:11–16*

I. Introduction
A. *The Church Is Ordained of God*
   1. The structure of local churches given in the Bible
   2. Officers and their duties are described
B. *Why Churches Often Move at a Snail's Pace*
   1. Pastors are carrying most of the load
   2. Members are not involved in ministry
C. *What Are a Pastor and Church to Do?*

II. Body
A. *The Pastor Is a Gift to the Church (v. 11)*
   1. This may come as a surprise
      a. Some think of the ministry as a profession
      b. Instead, it is a calling of God
   2. Some distinctions:
      a. The pastor is not an apostle
      b. The pastor is not a prophet
      c. Though not an evangelist, he must evangelize (2 Tim. 4:5)
   3. Pastors must teach by example and exhortation
   4. Pastors are undershepherds, feeding and leading the sheep
B. *The Pastor Must Perfect Believers for Ministry (v. 12)*
   1. What are the pastor's duties?
      a. They are many and varied
      b. Preaching, teaching, praying, studying, counseling
      c. He must set the pace in personal witnessing (2 Tim. 4:5)
   2. Most importantly, he must perfect the saints for ministry
      a. The church is not a one-man ministry
      b. He must train people to minister
   3. This multiplies the ministry of any church

C. *The Pastor and the Church Must Minister and Multiply (v. 12)*
   1. "For the edifying (building up) of the body of Christ"
   2. Both pastor and people become church builders
   3. See how this was true in the early church
      a. All believers involved at Pentecost (Acts 2:1–11)
      b. Praying, praising, learning, growing (Acts 2:41–47)
      c. They seized every opportunity to witness (Acts 8:4)
   4. "Like a mighty army moves the church of God"
      a. This is true when all are ministering
      b. Early Christians turned the world upside down (Acts 17:6)
      c. This is impossible with only leaders ministering
   5. Believers multiply when all minister
      a. Three thousand saved at Pentecost (Acts 2:41)
      b. Two thousand more when persecution began (Acts 4:4)
      c. Multitudes of converts added (Acts 5:14)
      d. From addition to multiplication (Acts 6:7)
   6. We must all get involved to be effective for Christ

III. Conclusion
  A. *Dynamic Results from Sticking to God's Instructions*
    1. Our church can be dynamite
    2. We can make a difference
    3. We can evangelize our community
    4. We can impact the world
  B. *Let's Follow God's Plan for the Church to Mature and Multiply*

Calling God's Man

2 Samuel 16:1–13

I. **Introduction**
   A. *The Important Task of Calling a Pastor*
      1. Calling, not hiring
      2. Important to find God's will
   B. *A Parallel: Samuel Goes to Choose a King*
      1. Told to anoint one of the sons of Jesse
      2. Not calling a king to the church, but some principles apply

II. **Body**
   A. *The Lord Sees the Real Personality of a Man (vv. 6–7)*
      1. The firstborn of Jesse seems to be the one
         a. Tall and handsome; appears perfect
         b. Reminds Samuel of Saul whom he had admired
      2. Pitfalls concerning the first man
         a. He may be passed over because he is first
         b. He may be called for fear another can't be found
      3. Only God knows the man of His choosing
         a. You only hear his best sermons
         b. You only see him at his best
         c. You are limited, but God is unlimited
      4. Some things to remember
         a. Choose a shepherd's heart over physical appearance
         b. Choose power in prayer over public relations
         c. Choose a strong devotional life over educational degrees
         d. Choose love for people over eloquence in speaking
         e. Choose concern for souls over administrative ability
   B. *The Lord Sees the Real Potential in a Man (vv. 7–11)*
      1. The Lord refuses all the sons of Jesse who are there
      2. How frustrating for Samuel!

     3. Never call a man because you are tired of looking
     4. Is there another?
        a. Just one, who is out tending sheep
        b. A good qualification for pastoring
     5. The youngest (David) is brought to Samuel
        a. Not much experience
        b. No impressive references
     6. Never refuse a man because of his age
     7. David didn't have much of a past, but a great future
        a. A man with God's song in his heart
        b. A man of prayer and praise
        c. A man who loves God's Word
        d. A man with prophetic insights

C. *The Lord Gives Peace Concerning the Right Man (vv. 12–13)*
     1. "Arise and anoint him"
     2. The Lord will show His praying people what to do
     3. Finding the Lord's will calls for prayer and persistence
     4. Calling a pastor should move a church to revival

III. Conclusion
    A. *A Church Should Pray Its Way to the Knowledge of God's Will*
    B. *Draw Near to God and He Will Lead You to His Man*
    C. *Let the Praying Begin*

The Superficial Thanksgiving

Thanksgiving   *Luke 18:9–14*

I. Introduction
    A. How Fitting to Have a National Day of Thanksgiving!
        1. "A good thing to give thanks" (Ps. 92:1)
        2. A. W. Tozer: "Thanksgiving has great curative powers."
        3. Let us thank our way to spiritual health
    B. But for Many This Week of Thanks Will Be Superficial
        1. For some a time of praise, for others a pretext
        2. For some a spiritual time, for others a superficial time
    C. The Pharisee and His Superficial Thanksgiving

II. Body
    A. The Pharisee Was Unaware of His Greatest Need (vv. 11–12)
        1. "I thank thee that I am not as other men"
        2. Started with thanksgiving but the wrong kind
        3. H. A. Ironside: "This man was not thanking God for what grace had done for him; he was thanking God for what he himself had done, and that is the wrong attitude."
        4. D. L. Moody: "It was a very prayerless prayer. He said a prayer but he didn't pray any."
        5. He focused on human efforts: dos and don'ts
        6. He needed personal salvation through faith in Christ
            a. Something he couldn't earn by his good works
            b. He could only receive it as a gift (Eph. 2:8–9)
    B. The Pharisee Was Unconcerned about the Publican (v. 11)
        1. "Or even this publican"
        2. The difference filled him with pride rather than compassion
        3. True thanksgiving produces thankful living
            a. Thankful for salvation? Tell others of Christ
            b. Thankful for provision? Share it with others
            c. Thankful for kindnesses? Pass them on

       d.   Thankful for Christian fellowship? Extend fellowship
       e.   Thankful for prayers? Pray for others
   4.   This is the spirit of the first Thanksgiving
       a.   They shared with one another
       b.   They were truly thankful

  C. *The Pharisee Was Unchanged When He Returned Home (v. 14)*
   1.   True thanksgiving changes us
   2.   He went to a good place: the temple
   3.   He went for a good purpose: to pray
   4.   He went home unchanged
   5.   Millions leave churches unchanged
   6.   Don't let this happen to you

III. **Conclusion**
  A. *The Other Person in This Parable: The Publican (vv. 13–14)*
   1.   This man faced his sins and sought forgiveness
   2.   Nothing superficial about his response
   3.   "God be merciful to me a sinner"
  B. *The Publican Went Home a New Man*
   1.   He went home forgiven: justified (v. 14)
   2.   Now he could be truly thankful
   3.   How about you?

One Thankful Man

Thanksgiving   *Luke 17:11–19*

I. **Introduction**
  A. *Thanksgiving in the Bible*
    1. Mentioned 140 times
    2. Thankful David (Ps. 103)
    3. Thankful Daniel (Dan. 6:10)
    4. Thankful Paul (1 Thess. 5:18)
  B. *Lessons on Thankfulness from a Leper*
    1. Jesus meets ten lepers
    2. One of them will soon be a thankful man

II. **Body**
  A. *The Lepers Call to Jesus (vv. 12–13)*
    1. When Jesus saw the lepers
      a. As He entered the village
      b. They stood afar off as was commanded (Lev. 13:46)
    2. Leprosy pictures the sinful state of us all
    3. "Jesus, Master, have mercy upon us"
      a. Our Lord is rich in mercy
      b. His mercies are new every morning (Lam. 3:22–23)
      c. They have called on the right Man
    4. These lepers had many things in common with us
      a. They were all afflicted with the same disease (Rom. 3:23)
      b. They were all dying men (Rom. 6:23)
      c. Without Christ, they had no hope (Eph. 2:11)
  B. *The Lepers Cleansed by Jesus (v. 14)*
    1. Our Lord's look of compassion: "when he saw them"
    2. Jesus responded to their call
    3. Why "Go, show yourselves to the priests"?
      a. His command demanded faith
      b. The priests had authority to pronounce them clean
      c. Christ's work stands the scrutiny of man

     4. As they went they were cleansed
        a. Their first step of faith brought cleansing
        b. Faith in Christ brings immediate cleansing
           from sin
     5. Will you take that step?

C. *The Leper Who Was Thankful (vv. 15–16)*
     1. Upon being healed he came back to Jesus
        a. He glorified God with a loud voice
        b. He fell down at the feet of Jesus
        c. He gave thanks
     2. Why the leper gave thanks
        a. He had been hopeless, now he had hope
        b. He had been homeless, now he could go home
        c. He had been rejected, now he would be
           received
     3. We ought to be as thankful as this cleansed leper

D. *The Lepers Who Were Thoughtless (vv. 17–18)*
     1. Nine cleansed lepers went on their way
     2. The sad words of Jesus: "Where are the nine?"
     3. How soon we forget the goodness of God!

III. Conclusion

A. *Jesus Commends a Thankful Man (v. 19)*
B. *Are We Thankful or Thoughtless?*
C. *Our Gracious Lord Deserves Thanksgiving and Praise*

Wonderful

Series on the Birth of Christ   *Isaiah 9:6*

I. Introduction

A. *Isaiah Concerning Jesus*
   1. Announced the birth of Jesus
   2. Wrote about the life of Jesus
   3. Described the death of Jesus
   4. Prophesied the coming kingdom of Jesus

B. *Isaiah's Revelation of Our Lord's Many Names*
   1. Wonderful, Counselor, the Mighty God, the Everlasting Father, the Prince of Peace
   2. Beginning a sermon series on these names

C. *His Name Shall Be Called Wonderful*

II. Body

A. *Jesus Was Wonderful in His Birth (Isa. 7:14)*
   1. "A virgin shall conceive"
      a. Isaiah's prophecy of the miraculous birth
      b. Gabriel's message to Mary (Luke 1:26–38)
      c. Mary's confusion and Gabriel's reassuring answer
   2. The Virgin Birth was a miracle
   3. Other miracles at His birth
      a. The angelic appearances (to Mary, Joseph, and shepherds)
      b. The taxing that brought them to Bethlehem (Mic. 5:2)
      c. The arrival of the wise men (Matt. 2)
   4. Don't try to explain the miracles of Christmas

B. *Jesus Was Wonderful in His Life (Isa. 32:2)*
   1. The wonderful baby in the manger was a miracle
      a. But Jesus is no longer in the manger
      b. The birth was only part of God's great plan
   2. We no longer worship a babe in a manger
   3. We worship the sinless Savior who meets people in crises
      a. He is like a hiding place from the wind
      b. He is like a covert from the tempest
      c. He is like rivers of water in a dry place
      d. He is like the shadow of a great rock in a weary land

    4. He will meet you in your crisis and deliver you

C. *Jesus Was Wonderful in His Death (Isa. 53)*
    1. All die because of sin (Heb. 9:27)
    2. Jesus was sinless and died for sinners (vv. 4–5)
        a. He died carrying our sorrows
        b. He died as our substitute
    3. All our sins were laid on Him (v. 6)

D. *Jesus Will Be Wonderful in His Coming Kingdom (Isa. 35)*
    1. The One who died and rose again will come again
    2. When He comes to reign the promise to Mary will be fulfilled
        a. He shall reign forever and ever
        b. Of His kingdom there will be no end

III. Conclusion

    A. *Is Jesus Wonderful to You?*
    B. *Trust Him and You Will Find Him Wonderful Too*

Counselor

Isaiah 9:6

I. **Introduction**
   A. *Isaiah's Early Announcement of the Birth of Jesus*
      1. Most birth announcements after the birth
      2. Isaiah gave his centuries before
   B. *Why So Many Names in This Announcement?*
      1. Many names needed to describe this wonderful One
      2. Names that reveal the personality of our Lord
   C. *His Name Shall Be Called Counselor*

II. **Body**
   A. *As Counselor He Became Available*
      1. The name "Counselor" speaks of His wisdom
      2. When wisdom is worthless
         a. When it is not available
         b. When it cannot be applied to life
      3. Jesus became available (Phil. 2:5–7)
         a. He came to the manger (Luke 2:1–7)
         b. His birth was announced to shepherds (Luke 2:8–14)
         c. Wise men came to worship Him (Matt. 2:1–11)
      4. Jesus was always available during His ministry
         a. Available to children and adults
         b. Available to rich and poor
         c. Available to sinners like you and me
   B. *As Counselor He Came with Answers*
      1. Answers for the doctors in the temple (Luke 2:41–52)
      2. Answers for Nicodemus, a ruler of the Jews (John 3)
      3. Answers for His critics (John 2:18–22)
      4. Answers about eternity
         a. The promise of heaven (John 14:1–6)
         b. The peril of hell (Luke 16:19–31)
   C. *As Counselor He Came with Assurance for Hopeless Sinners*
      1. He brought a message of love
         a. Love for the woman at the well (John 4)

191

       b. Love for crooked Zacchaeus (Luke 19:1–10)

       c. Love for a dying thief (Luke 23:39–43)

   2. Jesus brought hope to those who had no hope

   3. No problem was too difficult for Him to solve

       a. He still reaches out to those who have no hope

       b. He offers hope to you and me

III. Conclusion

   A. *We Celebrate More Than a Miracle Birth*

      1. This virgin-born Savior has the answers needed today

      2. Answers that are relevant to every need of every age

   B. *Bring Your Burdens and Problems to Him*

   C. *His Wise Counsel Will Guide You through Them All*

The Mighty God

Series on the Birth of Christ   *Isaiah 9:6*

I. **Introduction**
   A. *Isaiah Preparing Us for Christmas*
      1. His prophecy of the virgin birth (7:14)
      2. His revelation of the many names of Christ (9:6)
   B. *A Child to Be Born, a Son Given*
      1. A child who would someday govern
      2. Compare to Gabriel's word to Mary
         (Luke 1:30–33)
   C. *Why This Coming Son Was to Be Called the Mighty
      God*

II. **Body**
   A. *John the Baptist to Prepare the Way for the Mighty
      God (40:3–5)*
      1. The other miraculous birth
         a. Zacharias serving in the temple (Luke 1:5–10)
         b. Zacharias and Elisabeth childless (1:7)
         c. An angel announces the coming birth of John
            (1:13)
      2. This one to be born prophesied by Isaiah (40:3–5)
      3. John the Baptist to prepare the way of the Lord
         a. The One to come would exalt those in valleys
         b. He would bring the proud low
         c. He would make the crooked straight
         d. He would make the rough smooth
      4. Only the mighty God can work such miracles in
         people
      5. The mighty God at work in each of us through the
         Gospel
   B. *The Mighty God to Bring Light to Those in Darkness
      (Luke 1:76–79)*
      1. Jesus called the "Dayspring": the dawn
      2. John to be a prophet of the Highest
         a. He would give light to those in darkness
         b. He would give light to those in the shadow of
            death
         c. He would give guidance to those in trouble

193

   3. Human solutions for problems fail
   4. We need the wisdom of the mighty God

  C. *The Shepherds Were to Go and Find the Mighty God*
    (Luke 2:10–12)
   1. The first announcement was to common men
   2. A Savior: Christ the Lord
    a. "A Savior!" What good news for sinners!
    b. This Savior is Christ the Lord
   3. The shepherds went and found the Lord as directed
   4. Have you found Him to be the mighty God?

III. Conclusion
  A. *Come with All Your Sins to the One Who Is Mighty to*
    Save
  B. *Come with All Your Problems to the One Who Is*
    Mighty to Solve
  C. *The Mighty God Awaits Your Call; Trust Him with*
    Your Life, Your All

The Everlasting Father

Series on the Birth of Christ   *Isaiah 9:6*

I. **Introduction**
   A. *Celebrating Christmas in the Old Testament*
      1. Isaiah saw it all in advance
      2. From the Virgin Birth to the coming kingdom
   B. *The Dimensions of Deity*
      1. The names of our Lord to describe His character
      2. Wonderful, Counselor, the mighty God
      3. More than a birth: the Incarnation
   C. *What Does the Everlasting Father Imply?*

II. **Body**
   A. *The Everlasting One Entered Time*
      1. Why Jesus had to be born in Bethlehem
         a. Required by the prophecy of Micah (5:2)
         b. The everlasting One must enter time there
      2. Why Bethlehem was chosen
         a. First mention: place of Rachel's death
            (Gen. 35:15–20)
            (1) A place of sorrows
            (2) Jesus to be a Man of Sorrows
         b. The place of David's birth and anointing
            (1 Sam. 16)
         c. *Bethlehem-Ephratah* means "house of bread"
            (1) Jesus is the bread of life (John 6:35)
            (2) He satisfies hungry souls
      3. The Savior's future and past
         a. "To be ruler in Israel" (v. 2)
         b. "From of old, from everlasting" (v. 2)
   B. *The Everlasting One Made Himself Subject to Time*
      1. The miracles of the Incarnation (Phil. 2:5–7)
         a. Our Lord's pre-incarnate position (v. 6)
         b. Made Himself of no reputation (v. 7)
         c. Took upon Himself the form of a servant (v. 7)
         d. Made in the likeness of men (v. 7)
         e. Humbled Himself and died on the cross for us (v. 8)
      2. In all this, He became subject to time
         a. He was born at a particular time (Luke 2:1–7)

195

        b.   He experienced growth over time (Luke 2:52)

        c.   In birth and death, He was on time
           (Gal. 4:4–6)

    3.   Now He's alive forevermore (Heb. 7:25; Rev. 1:8)

  C. *The Subjects of Time Are Offered Eternal Life*

    1.   We are subjects of time

        a.   At birth, we begin to age

        b.   Time takes it toll on us all

        c.   We leave life much as we came

    2.   By faith in Christ we receive everlasting life
        (John 3:16)

III. **Conclusion**

  A. *What Will You Do with God's Offer of Everlasting*
     Life?

  B. *Receive It by Faith While You Have Time*

The Prince of Peace

Isaiah 9:6

I. **Introduction**
   A. *A Prince Was Born in Bethlehem*
      1. The "Prince of life" (Acts 3:15)
      2. The "Prince of the kings of the earth" (Rev. 1:5)
      3. The "Prince of Peace" (Isa. 9:6)
   B. *Three Dimensions of Peace*
      1. Peace with God
      2. The peace of God
      3. Peace on earth

II. **Body**
   A. *Peace with God (Rom. 5:1)*
      1. Millions have sought peace with God
         a. Through religious ritual
         b. Through good works
         c. Through giving money or possessions
      2. The great gulf between sinners and our Holy God
      3. The gulf bridged by the cross
         a. He paid our debt of sin (Isa. 53:5–6)
         b. He broke down all barriers (Eph. 2:12–18)
         c. He made peace through His blood (Col. 1:20)
      4. We find peace with God through faith in Jesus (Rom. 5:1)
   B. *The Peace of God (Phil. 4:5–8)*
      1. Peace with God is positional and unchanging
      2. The peace of God is dependent on our relationship with Him
      3. Many have peace with God but miss the peace of God
      4. The path to peace
         a. Be anxious about nothing (v. 6)
         b. Pray about everything (v. 6)
         c. Give thanks without ceasing (v. 6)
         d. Think only about praise (v. 8)
      5. The result: peace that passes understanding

    C. *Peace on Earth (Isa. 2:4)*
      1. "Peace on earth good will toward men"
        (Luke 2:14)
      2. This peace awaits the kingdom
        a. No more war (v. 4)
        b. Even peace among animals (Isa. 11:6–8)
        c. Peace instead of violence (Isa. 11:9–10)
        d. Peace in nature (Isa. 35:1–2, 7)
      3. Gabriel's promises to Mary fulfilled
        (Luke 1:30–33)
      4. The best is yet to come

III. Conclusion
    A. *Do You Long for Peace?*
    B. *Christ Will Bring Peace to Your Troubled Heart*
    C. *Someday He Will Bring Peace to This Troubled World*

The Wonders of Christmas

Series on the Birth of Christ   *Luke 2:1–14*

I. Introduction
    A. *Christmas Is a Season of Wonders*
       1. The wonder of the birth of Jesus
       2. The wonder of beautiful music
       3. The wonder of giving and receiving gifts
       4. The wonder of children with happy faces
    B. *Some Lose the Wonder*
       1. Has this happened to you?
       2. Has the rush of the season cost you the wonder?
       3. Gypsy Smith: "I have never lost the wonder of it all"
    C. *The Wonder of the Characters of Christmas*

II. Body
    A. *The Wonder of the Angels Moved Them to Glory (v. 14)*
       1. Angels played important roles in the birth of Jesus
         a. The appearance to Zacharias (Luke 1:5–20)
         b. The appearance of Gabriel to Mary (Luke 1:26–38)
         c. The appearance to Joseph (Matt. 1:18–25)
         d. The announcement to the shepherds (2:8–14)
       2. A multitude of angels gave glory to God
         a. "Glory to God" was not a new song for angels
         b. But "In the highest" was an added line
       3. Higher in glory God could not go
         a. The Gospel declares God's highest glory
         b. When a soul is saved, angels glory again (Luke 15:10)
    B. *The Wonder of the Shepherds Moved Them to Go (vv. 15, 20)*
       1. The good news given to these humble men (vv. 8–12)
       2. Imagine being one of them
         a. You have lived through a routine day
         b. The sheep are settling down for the night
         c. You sit and talk about common things
         d. Suddenly uncommon things happen

      3. An angel appears; God has your attention
      4. The wonderful message: Christ is born
         a. The response: "Let us now go" (v. 15)
         b. After finding Jesus they went to tell others
      5. They shared the wonder

C. *The Wonder of the Wise Men Moved Them to Give
   (Matt. 2:11)*
      1. The most mysterious characters of Christmas
         a. Not sure where they came from
         b. Not sure how many there were
         c. Not sure just when they arrived
      2. We are sure that they gave gifts to Jesus
         a. This was why they had left their homes
         b. They gave their treasures
      3. George Müller: "Giving is not measured by what
         you give but by what you have left."

III. Conclusion
   A. *What Has the Wonder of Christ's Birth Moved You to
     Do?*
   B. *Ask God to Restore the Wonder*
   C. *Get on the Move for Him*

Simeon and His Secret

Series on the Birth of Christ   *Luke 2:21–35*

I. **Introduction**
   A. *Looking Back to Christmas Day*
      1. Was the family together?
      2. Was Jesus the center of your celebration?
   B. *What Follows Christmas?*
      1. Are you still thrilled with Jesus?
      2. Are you more dedicated to Him?
   C. *Encounter with Simeon after the Manger Birth*
      1. The presentation of Jesus in the temple
      2. The circumcision and naming of Jesus
      3. The meeting with Simeon (v. 25)

II. **Body**
   A. *A Portrait of Simeon (vv. 25–27)*
      1. What we know about him:
         a. He lived in Jerusalem
         b. He was a just man
         c. He was devout (warmly devoted, sincere)
      2. Others who are called devout
         a. Jews gathered for Pentecost (Acts 2:5)
         b. Those who carried Stephen to his burial
            (Acts 8:2)
         c. Cornelius (Acts 10:2)
         d. Ananias, who prayed for Saul (Acts 22:12)
      3. We know Simeon longed for the Savior to come
      4. We know he was led by the Holy Spirit
         a. A man God could trust with secrets
         b. He knew he would live until Jesus was born
            (v. 26)
   B. *The Prayer of Simeon (vv. 28–32)*
      1. He took Jesus up in his arms
      2. Someday Jesus will take us up in His arms
      3. His prayer involves satisfaction (v. 29)
      4. His prayer involves salvation (v. 30)
      5. His prayer involves God's sovereignty (v. 31)
      6. His prayer involves both Jews and Gentiles (v. 32)

201

C. *The Prophecy of Simeon (vv. 34–35)*
1. The fall and rising again of many in Israel
    a. Jesus a stumbling block to many
    b. But many who stumble later rise up to trust Him
2. A sign which shall be spoken against
    a. How this was fulfilled in His life
    b. How this was fulfilled in His trial and crucifixion
    c. How this is true among many today
3. A sword shall pierce thine own soul also
    a. Mary and others at the cross
    b. The thoughts of many revealed at the cross

III. Conclusion

A. *Are You Living Close Enough to Jesus to Know His Secrets?*
B. *Are You Aware of His Plan for This Age?*
C. *Are You Aware of His Plan for Your Life?*

Rich Man—Poor Man

Series on the Birth of Christ   *2 Corinthians 8:9*

I. **Introduction**
   A. *New Testament Contributors to the Christmas Account*
      1. Matthew wrote of Christ the King (the royal line)
      2. Luke wrote of Christ the Son of Man (born in a stable)
      3. John wrote of the deity of Christ (the Word made flesh)
      4. Paul condensed Christmas to one rich revelation
   B. *The Cost of Christmas*
      1. Our rich Savior became poor
      2. He did this that we might become rich

II. **Body**
   A. *What the Savior Laid Aside When He Became Poor*
      1. "Though He was rich . . . He became poor"
      2. He laid aside His place in heaven
         a. A place of perfect climate; of perfect citizens
         b. A place of continual praise; of perpetual peace
         c. Some won't even leave a comfortable bed to worship Him
      3. He laid aside His position in heaven (Phil. 2:5–7)
         a. He left the worship of angels
         b. He came to the rejection of the innkeeper
         c. Some so occupied with position they won't serve Him
   B. *Why the Savior Became Poor*
      1. "For your sakes"
      2. No wonder shepherds must be notified immediately
      3. No wonder wise men must be guided by a star
      4. Everything in the humiliation of Christ is for our sakes
         a. He left heaven so we can go to heaven
         b. He was rejected so we will never be rejected
         c. He was born in a stable so we can be born of the Spirit
         d. He became a servant so we can become saints
         e. He died so we can have eternal life

203

C. *What the Savior Gives to Poor Sinners to Make Them
    Rich*
    1. "Might be rich"
    2. Great gifts from Jesus that make us rich
        a. The gift of salvation (Eph. 2:8–9)
        b. The gift of eternal life (Rom. 6:23)
        c. The gift of the Holy Spirit (Rom. 5:5)
        d. The gift of righteousness (Rom. 5:17–18)
        e. The gift of peace (John 14:17)
        f. The gift of victory over death (1 Cor. 15:57)

III.   **Conclusion**
    A. *Come to Christ as a Poor Sinner*
    B. *Receive These Rich Gifts from His Hand*
    C. *Why Delay When Eternal Riches Can Be Yours?*

Turning the World Upside Down

Acts 17:6

I. **Introduction**
   A. *Our Debt to the Early Church*
      1. They evangelized their world
      2. They took the Great Commission seriously (Matt. 28:18–20)
      3. They were faithful so we have the message today
   B. *Their Challenge and Ours*
      1. Christians a minority compared to the world
      2. Christians commissioned to reach the world
      3. People being born faster than reborn
   C. *What Did Those Early Christians Have That We Need?*

II. **Body**
   A. *They Were on Fire for Christ (Acts 2:3)*
      1. "Cloven tongues as of fire"
         a. Evidence of the Holy Spirit working through them
         b. The effect: souls won, churches planted
      2. The world needs to see the church on fire
         a. Not enough to be fundamental; must be on fire
         b. Not enough to be doctrinally sound; may be sound asleep
         c. Not enough to be preaching; must be pleading
         d. Not enough to be Bible believing; must be burning
      3. David Dawson: "So afraid of wild fire, we have settled for no fire at all."
   B. *They Found True Fellowship in Christ (Acts 2:41–46)*
      1. "In fellowship, and in breaking of bread, and in prayers"
      2. Once divided, now bound together in love
      3. The basis of their fellowship: the apostles doctrine
         a. They based their fellowship on truth
         b. They celebrated the Gospel in daily life
      4. Do we have that kind of fellowship?
      5. What are we going to do to achieve it?

 C. *They Were Fully Surrendered to Christ (Acts 4:18–20)*
  1. "We cannot but speak"
  2. They laid everything on the altar
   a. To some this meant financial loss
   b. To some this meant prison
   c. To some this meant martyrdom
   d. No wonder they were effective
  3. Too many Christians trying to save their lives
   a. As a result they lose them (Matt. 16:25)
   b. They lose also their impact for Christ

III. Conclusion
 A. *Our Need of Genuine Revival*
 B. *The Example of New Testament Believers Could Produce It*
  1. Do we long for their fire and fellowship?
  2. Are we willing to make their kind of surrender?

Triumphant in Trouble

Psalm 3

I. **Introduction**
   A. *The Setting of the Psalm*
      1. Absalom's revolt against David
      2. What could be more difficult to bear?
   B. *A Psalm That Meets Us in Times of Trouble*
      1. Many experience family problems
      2. Gossip and criticism are common sources of grief
      3. Friends sometimes turn against us

II. **Body**
   A. *The Lord Is Our Shield (v. 3)*
      1. The arrows and spears of David's time
      2. The fiery darts of Satan we endure (Eph. 6:16)
      3. God's people have always been targets of enemies
      4. But God is our shield
         a. Abraham's shield (Gen. 15:1)
         b. David's shield (3:3; 33:20; 84:11)
      5. The shield protects during battle
   B. *The Lord Is Our Sustainer (vv. 4–5)*
      1. David cried out to the Lord for help
      2. Our Lord's many invitations to pray
         a. "Call unto me" (Jer. 33:3)
         b. "Ask and it shall be given" (Matt. 7:7)
         c. "Believe that ye receive" (Mark 11:24)
         d. "Ask what ye will" (John 15:7)
      3. David had such peace that he could sleep (v. 5)
         a. He slept in peace and awoke invigorated
         b. The Lord sustained him in danger
   C. *The Lord Is Our Strength (v. 6)*
      1. "I will not be afraid"
         a. Consider the circumstances
         b. The forces against him
      2. One plus God is a majority
      3. As faith increases, fear decreases
      4. Perfect love casts out fear (1 John 4:18)
   D. *The Lord Is Our Source of Victory (vv. 7–8)*
      1. David sees his enemies overcome by God's power

207

  2. Salvation is of the Lord
     a. Our salvation is also of the Lord
     b. Salvation from our sins by Christ's blood
        (Rom. 5:6–9)
     c. Victory during Satan's attacks (Eph. 6:10–18)
  3. There really is victory in Jesus (1 Cor. 15:57–58)

III. Conclusion
   A. *We Can Rest in Christ Even in Troubled Times*
   B. *The Lord Is Our Shield, Our Sustainer, Our Strength,*
      Our Salvation

Family Ties

Hebrews 10:22–25

I. Introduction
   A. *One of the Most Encouraging Texts in the Bible*
   B. *A Text Preceded by Great News*
      1. Forgiveness is available (v. 17)
      2. The blood of Christ is sufficient (v. 19)
      3. Christ is our great high priest (v. 21)
   C. *A Text for the Family of God*
      1. "Let us" speaks of fellowship in the body of Christ
      2. Ties earthly fellowship to heavenly anticipation

II. Body
   A. *We Are Drawn Together in the Same Assurance (v. 22)*
      1. "Let us draw near in full assurance"
      2. *Assurance*: What a good word!
         a. A word that removes all doubts
         b. A word that eliminates uncertainty
      3. Our Lord wants us to have "full assurance" (v. 14)
      4. A true heart is filled with assurance by faith (vv. 35–39)
      5. The blood of Christ purges the believer's conscience (9:14)
   B. *We Are Held Together in the Same Hope (v. 23)*
      1. "Let us hold fast the profession of our faith"
         a. Believing our beliefs
         b. Doubting our doubts
      2. Here is unwavering confidence
         a. Based on the finished work of Christ (9:28)
         b. Resting on His resurrection and return (9:28)
      3. Sins are forgiven and heaven is sure
   C. *We Are Working Together in the Same Love (v. 24)*
      1. "Let us consider one another"
      2. Note the sequence: faith, hope, love (1 Cor. 13)
      3. Love is considerate of others
         a. Love's consideration provokes more love
         b. Love's consideration provokes to good works
         c. How love affects any congregation
            (Acts 2:41–46)

    D. We Meet Together in the Same Anticipation (v. 25)
       1. "Not forsaking the assembling . . ."
       2. The importance of believers gathering for worship
       3. We need each other
          a. We meet to exhort (encourage) one another
          b. We find comfort in our Lord's return
       4. Some will neglect gathering as Christ's coming approaches
          a. Christ's return should make us eager to gather
          b. Jesus may come today

III. Conclusion
    A. What Can We Do to Strengthen the Family?
    B. The Family Functions Best When We Are All Faithful

The Unconquerable Church

Revelation 2:8–11

I. **Introduction**
  A. *Jesus Writes to a Suffering Church*
    1. The second of seven letters
    2. The shortest of seven letters
  B. *A Letter for Sufferers of All Time*

II. **Body**
  A. *A Church That Was Triumphant While Troubled (v. 9)*
    1. "I know thy . . . tribulation"
    2. Jesus knows all about our troubles
    3. We all experience trouble
      a. Most go through things they didn't think they would
      b. Many go through things they didn't think they could
    4. Trouble foretold: "Ye shall have tribulation" (John 16:33)
      a. Physical trouble (the early persecutions)
      b. Emotional trouble (suffering and death of loved ones)
    5. Jesus presents Himself as the One they need in trouble
      a. The first and the last: our future secure in Him
      b. The One who was dead and is alive: crucified and risen
  B. *A Church That Was Rich While Poor (v. 9)*
    1. "I know thy . . . poverty"
    2. This group was poor as a church
      a. No great temples, plush carpets, tall steeples
      b. In the eyes of God they were rich
    3. The people were poor as individuals
      a. Barely enough to survive
      b. Through faith they had eternal riches
    4. Consider our opportunities for lasting riches
      a. Rich in our position in Christ (2 Cor. 8:9)
      b. Rich in works for Christ (1 Tim. 6:18)

           c. Rich when sharing the reproach of Christ (Heb. 11:26)

           d. Rich in faith (James 2:5)

   C. *A Church That Was Faithful While Suffering (v. 10)*

      1. "Fear none of those things which thou shalt suffer"

      2. All believers suffer to some degree (2 Tim. 3:12)

      3. Consider the suffering of the early church

         a. All the apostles except John were martyred

         b. Intense suffering by many believers

           (1) Polycarp burned at the stake

           (2) Ignatius cast to the lions

           (3) Some tortured to death by dogs

           (4) Some crucified, waxed, or burned

      4. Be faithful to death

         a. Not—until ridiculed

         b. Not—until tired or discouraged

III. Conclusion

   A. *Rewards for Overcomers*

      1. A crown of life

      2. Not to be hurt by the second death

   B. *Serving Christ Brings True Rewards*

Glory to God

I. **Introduction**
   A. *A Psalm of Glory*
      1. Begins with the heavens glorifying God
      2. Ends with man glorifying God
   B. *A Psalm of Praise*
      1. The praise of creation (v. 1)
      2. The praise of inspiration (vv. 7–8)
      3. The praise of a consecrated heart (v. 14)

II. **Body**
   A. *Creation's Glory (vv. 1–6)*
      1. Every time we look up we see God's glory
         a. Compare this with Psalm 8
         b. Both psalms declare God's glory
         c. Both psalms remind us of our need of Him
      2. Man's mistake in worshipping the heavens
         a. True from earliest times (Rom. 1:20–25)
         b. True in man's present search of the heavens
      3. Day and night remind us of the Creator
      4. Creation's witness leaves the world without excuse (Rom. 1:20)
      5. The sun reminds us of the Son, the Bridegroom
   B. *Inspiration's Glory (vv. 7–11)*
      1. God's perfect law makes us see the need of conversion
      2. The testimony of the Lord brings wisdom
      3. The statutes of the Lord rejoice our hearts
      4. The commandments of the Lord enlighten our eyes
      5. Man's present search for his origin in the heavens
         a. Creation's lessons never contradict inspiration
         b. The Scriptures have already revealed our origin
         c. Nothing will be found to prove them wrong
   C. *Consecration's Glory (vv. 12–14)*
      1. Considering God's glory brings conviction of sin
      2. We then grasp the great gap between God and man

 3. The desire to bridge the gap
   a. Who can understand his errors?
   b. Cleanse me from secret faults
   c. Keep me from presumptuous sins (prideful, rebellious)
 4. The great prayer of consecration
   a. The psalmist wants his words to please God
   b. He even wants his thoughts to please God
   c. A good prayer for every day
   d. A prayer concerning redemption, God's highest glory

III. Conclusion
 A. *Here Is Triune Glory: Creation, Inspiration, Consecration*
 B. *Wise Ones Live to the Glory of God*

This Man Receives Sinners

Luke 15:1–2

I. Introduction
- A. *The Amazing Observations of Christ's Enemies*
  1. Some of the most interesting statements in the Bible
     - a. "He saved others, himself he cannot save" (Mark 15:31)
     - b. "After three days, I will rise again" (Matt. 27:63)
     - c. "This man receiveth sinners"
- B. *Our Lord's Reaction to the Criticism of His Enemies*
  1. Jesus gives three parables about reaching sinners
  2. These parables show His compassion for the lost
- C. *Consider Some Reasons for This Criticism*

II. Body
- A. *Christ Was Truly a Man*
  1. "This man" (v. 2)
  2. God truly became man to redeem man (Gal. 4:4–7)
  3. The Savior first promised as a man
     - a. The seed of the woman (Gen. 3:15)
     - b. The Virgin Birth (Isa. 7:14)
     - c. Isaiah and the promised man (9:6; 32:2)
  4. As a man He enters into our pain
     - a. His humiliation (Phil. 2:5–7)
     - b. His temptation (Matt. 4; Luke 4)
     - c. His fatigue and thirst (John 4:6–7)
     - d. His sorrow (Isa. 53:3)
- B. *Christ Was Different from Sinful Men*
  1. "This man . . . sinners" (v. 2)
  2. He was different in many ways
     - a. In relation to His Father
     - b. In overcoming all temptation
     - c. In always doing His Father's will
  3. He was holy; without sin (Heb. 7:24–28)

    C. *Christ Was Always Reaching Out to Sinners*
        1.   "Receiveth sinners and eateth with them"
        2.   He came to seek and save that which was lost (Luke 19:10)
        3.   The parables that followed:
            a.   The lost sheep
            b.   The lost coin
            c.   The lost son

III. **Conclusion**
    A. *Christ Still Seeks Sinners*
        1.   He still receives them (John 6:37)
        2.   He still eats with them (Rev. 3:20)
    B. *Will You Join Him in Reaching Out to Sinners Every Day?*

Great Is Thy Faithfulness

I. **Introduction**
   A. *Lamentations: A Book of Trouble and Tears*
      1. We can identify with this many times in life
      2. In this world we have tribulation
   B. *God's Faithfulness Is Demonstrated in Tough Times*
      1. He was faithful to Israel in slavery
      2. He was faithful to Daniel in the den of lions
      3. Jeremiah finds hope: God is faithful

II. **Body**
   A. *The Lord Is Faithful in All Conditions (vv. 18–21)*
      1. Jeremiah's lament over the downfall of his people
         a. The chastening of God upon them
         b. The fall, the captivity (Ch. 1)
         c. No one seemed to care (1:12)
      2. We can share Jeremiah's tears
         a. The moral condition of our land
         b. Crime, drugs, immorality rampant
         c. The cold condition of the churches
      3. But there is a message of triumph in this book of tears
      4. There is a burst of delight in this book of despair
         a. God is faithful even when things look dark
         b. God's faithfulness revives His weeping prophet
   B. *The Lord Is Faithful in Mercy and Compassion (vv. 22–23)*
      1. *Mercy*: What a good word!
         a. A word that brings hope to troubled people
         b. A word that brings light to those in darkness
      2. *Compassion*: a word of comfort
         a. Compassion let's me feel as you feel
         b. Better still: God feels what we feel
         c. Reminds us of the good Samaritan
         d. Reminds us of Jesus and the hurting multitudes
      3. Note: "Mercies" and "Compassions"
         a. God's mercies and compassions reach to you and me

        b. He meets us in our sins and sorrows
        c. The publican's prayer: "God be merciful to me, a sinner"
  C. *The Lord Is Faithful to All Who Place Confidence in Him (vv. 24–26)*
    1. "I will hope in Him"
    2. "The Lord is good"
        a. To them that wait for Him
        b. To the soul that seeketh Him
    3. We can quietly wait for the salvation of the Lord

III. Conclusion
  A. *God Will Meet You with Mercy and Compassion Right Now*
  B. *Seek Him, Wait for Him, Hope in Him*
  C. *Trust Him*

God's Love and Our Losses

John 11:1–45

I. Introduction
   A. *We All Experience Times of Great Loss*
      1. Losses are part of life
      2. Our greatest losses are of loved ones
      3. Every family goes through the valley of the shadow of death
      4. "It is appointed unto man once to die" (Heb. 9:27)
   B. *God's Love Reaches Out to Broken Hearts*
      1. Whatever your loss, God understands
      2. When your heart is breaking, God cares
      3. The cross proves His love
   C. *Jesus and His Love for a Grieving Family*

II. Body
   A. *God's Love Brings Him to Where We Are (vv. 1–32)*
      1. The powerful ministry of Jesus beyond Jordan (10:39–42)
      2. The message that Lazarus is sick (11:1–3)
      3. Jesus loved Martha, Mary, and Lazarus (v. 5)
      4. His love caused Him to go where they were
         a. He left heaven to come where we are
         b. He endured the cross to come where we are
         c. He offers forgiveness, meeting us where we are
      5. Jesus met Martha and Mary with a message of life (vv. 23–32)
      6. His message to each of us is one of eternal life
   B. *God's Love Causes Him to Enter into Our Pain (vv. 33–38)*
      1. Entering the house of mourning
      2. Jesus feeling the pain of this grieving family
         a. He groaned in spirit (v. 33)
         b. He was troubled (v. 33)
         c. He wept (v. 35)
         d. He groaned in Himself (v. 36)
      3. Those present were aware of His love (v. 36)
      4. What compassion! What love!

   C. *God's Love Moves Him to Bring Us Hope (vv. 39–44)*
      1. Preparing for the resurrection of Lazarus
        a. The disciples will have a part
        b. "Take ye away the stone" (v. 39)
      2. The power of Christ over the grave
        a. "Lazarus, come forth" (v. 43)
        b. Lazarus responds to the Lord's call
      3. The disciples are to set him free
      4. Believers have a part in converts taking off grave-clothes
      5. We will be resurrected at the Lord's return
        (1 Thess. 4:13–18)

III. Conclusion
   A. *Our Loving Lord Invites Us to Bring Him Our Sins and Sorrows*
   B. *Respond to God's Call of Love and Find New Life in Him*

Scripture Index